Starting A Ministry

The Essential Roadmap When Building
a Thriving, Sustainable Ministry

"*A Work in Progress*"

© 2024, 2019 by John D. Leavy
All rights reserved.

Reproduction or translation of any part of this work beyond that permitted by Section 107 or 108 of the 1976 United States Copyright Act without permission of the copyright owner is unlawful. Requests for permission or further information should be emailed to: John D. Leavy at johndleavy@gmail.com.

This publication is designed to provide accurate and authoritative information regarding the subject matter covered. It is sold with the understanding that the publisher or author are not engaged in rendering legal, accounting or other professional services. If legal advice or other expert assistance is required, the services of a competent professional person should be sought.

ISBN-13:
978-1798108215 (John D. Leavy)

ISBN-10:
1798108216

Second Edition: July 2024
Printed in the United States of America

Starting A Ministry

> *"If you will look to God for help, and you seek the favor of the Almighty, and if you keep yourself pure and live with integrity, God will rouse himself on your behalf. And even though you started with little, you will end up with very much!*
>
> Job 8:5-7

Starting A Ministry

Table of Contents

Introduction 9

1: Stayin' Alive—The Balancing Act 13
2: Calling—What's Your Why? 18
3: Foundational—Turning Your Passion into Purpose 28
4: Market Research—Doing Your Homework 40
5: Compliance—Getting, Staying Legit 48
6: Personnel—Readying the Team 54
7: Insurance—Gotcha Covered 73
8: Budgeting—Counting the Cost 75
9: Branding—Looking Good 82
10: Marketing—Crafting Your Message 87
11: Public Relations—Being Seen in All the Right Places ... 92
12: Communication—Talking the Talk 100
13: Engagement—Walking the Walk 110
14: Development—Making New Friends 119
15: Fundraising—It's Not About the Money 126
16: Goal Setting—Dream Big! 135
17: Storytelling—Sharing Your Passion 157
18: Strategy—Planning Your Ground Game 166
19: Analysis—Are We There Yet? 175
20: Coaching— "I've Got Your Back" 197
21: Conclusion—Before I Go 204

Starting A Ministry

34 Example Worksheets

You're not on this journey alone. These examples and worksheets will help get you started on building a thriving, sustainable ministry.

The Four Question Worksheet
The Seven Question Worksheet
Statement of Purpose Worksheet
Vision Statement Worksheet
Mission Statement Worksheet
Doing Your Homework Worksheet
Volunteer Application Worksheet
Board Member Application Worksheet
Sample Board Meeting Agenda
Sample Board Meeting Minutes
Public Relations Worksheet
Communication Plan by Donor Schedule Example
Communication Plan by Channel Example
Engagement Strategy Worksheet
Relationship Building Quiz
Ministry X Goal Setting Example
Ministry Y Goal Setting Example
Ministry Z Goal Setting Example
S.M.A.R.T. Goal Setting Worksheet

Ministry X Project Priority Example
Ministry Y Project Priority Example
Ministry Z Project Priority Example
Project Priority Worksheet
Telling a Great Story Worksheet
Ministry X Action Plan Schedule Example
Ministry Y Action Plan Schedule Example
Ministry Z Action Plan Schedule Example
Action Plan Schedule Worksheet
Ministry X Traffic, Conversions, Average Gift Sizes Example
Ministry Y Traffic, Conversions, Average Gift Sizes Example
Ministry Z Traffic, Conversions, Average Gift Sizes Example
Traffic, Conversions, Average Gift Sizes Worksheet
Ministry X Measuring Your Progress Example
Ministry Y Measuring Your Progress Example
Ministry Z Measuring Your Progress Example
Measuring Your Progress Worksheet
Coaching Expectations Questionnaire

Introduction

Nothing kills a person's passion quicker than stress and strain piled on by anxiety and the fear of failure. **Starting A Ministry** is specifically designed to neutralize those negative feelings. It's a practical guidebook for starting a ministry on the right foot by laying a solid foundation.

Ministries have loads of moving parts. **Starting A Ministry** divides the startup tasks into two essential groups: those responsibilities that come first and those that should follow not long after. If you believe fundraising is hampering your ministry from moving forward, read **Chapter 15: Fundraising—It's Not About the Money** now and return to the balance of the book later.

Starting A Ministry covers all the steps a ministry leader needs to execute to achieve a solid, sustainable ministry model. **1: Stayin' Alive—The Balancing Act** talks about how a ministry must balance the operational, fundraising, and "calling" elements to be successful. **2: Calling—What's Your Why?** Make sure your passion is not misplaced. **3: Foundational—Turning Your Passion into Purpose** helps you construct the all-important Purpose, Vision, and Mission statements. **4: Market Research—Doing Your Homework** outlines how to perform the critical task of gathering client information. **5: Compliance—Getting Legit, Staying Legit** talks about the importance of forming a legal entity and staying compliant with the various government entities. **6: Personnel—Readying the Team** takes the reader through choosing the best possible candidates, whether for the board, leadership positions, staff, or volunteers. **7: Insurance—Gotcha Covered** highlights the need for insuring board members and officers against liabilities. **8: Budgeting—Counting the Cost** deals with the how-tos of constructing a workable ministry budget. **9: Branding—Looking Good** helps create a unique look that separates your ministry. **10: Marketing—Crafting Your Message** helps you craft messages that cause donors to act. **11: Public Relations—Being Seen in All the Right Places** talks about the merits of raising awareness of what the ministry is accomplishing. **12: Communication—Talking the Talk** outlines how choosing the correct tactic to communicate with one's donor audience makes all the difference. **13: Engagement—Walking the Walk** discusses ways to create two-way communication strategies. **14: Development—Cultivating Relationships** highlights the importance of creating cultivation strategies that move potential supporters through decision-making. **15: Fundraising—It's Not About the Money** takes the reader through building solid, productive fundraising approaches. **16: Goal Setting—Dream Big!** ensures the ministry objectives are not fuzzy and vague but specific, measurable, attainable, relevant, and time-bound. **17: Storytelling—Sharing Your Passion** reviews the nine ingredients that make a story great. **18: Strategy—Planning Your Ground Game** ensures all the moving parts are in the right place and working to capacity. **19: Analysis—Are We There Yet?**

emphasizes the significance of knowing whether the ministry is progressing towards its goals.

You'll find two bonus chapters, **20: Coaching— "I've Got You're Your Back."** this section summarizes what coaching brings: clarity, strategy, reinforcement, direction, and movement. **21: Conclusion—Before I Go** concludes with a few final thoughts of encouragement and cheering the ministry leaders on to success.

A Practical Application

Every ministry wants answers to these nine questions:

1. What is it we want to accomplish? (goals)
2. How will we know when we've arrived? (metrics)
3. Who's the target audience? (potential donors)
4. How do we share our passion? (message)
5. Who's going to do what? (people)
6. What tactics will be employed? (strategy)
7. What will the strategy cost? (funds)
8. When do the activities take place? (timetable)
9. Are we there yet? (measure progress)

Starting A Ministry does more than answer these nine essential questions; it takes the reader through valuable examples.

As a practical application, we'll take three made-up ministries (their names are Ministries X, Y, and Z) through these nine all-important questions and show how all the various elements work together.

For instance, to answer Question 1, we'll build goal-setting examples for all three organizations. To answer Question 6, we'll build example spreadsheets of the various tactics deployed. And to answer Question 8, we'll construct timetables.

 Starting A Ministry is loaded with 72 practical tips. Watch for the thumbs-up icon.

Read On!

John Leavy
johndleavy@gmail.com

– 1 –

Stayin' Alive:
The Balancing Act

What You'll Learn:

- **Learn** how to balance the demands (Operational, Fundraising, and The Calling) of running a thriving ministry.

A healthy, thriving ministry must understand that balance is the key to success. Realistically, an organization cannot devote 100% of its effort to "The Calling." Systems in place, the organization must be legal, volunteers enlisted, responsibilities assigned, goals set, plans made, donors identified and cultivated, and funds raised.

At different times in the organization's life, the tasks mentioned above are the most essential items that need attention.

The items that demand the most attention when starting a ministry are not the same ones that need one's devotion as the ministry grows and matures. The items that are most instrumental at the start are not the same as those that need watching when running or growing the organization.

Let's divide all the ministry actions into three categories. We'll call them operations, fundraising, and "The Calling."

Operation tasks include administration, management, branding, marketing, communication, and engagement. Fundraising involves acquiring the names of potential supporters, building relationships, and raising funds. "The Calling" is seen as the work on the ground. It's the ministry's "why."

Suppose we devote 100% of our time to these activities: operations, fundraising, and "The Calling," regardless of whether we devote a part-time or full-time effort.

Imagine we're looking at balancing operations, fundraising, and "The Calling" much the way one balances one's life. Some would say a balanced life includes: 1.) a healthy diet, 2.) exercise, 3.) sleep and rest, 4.) mind, 5.) relationships, and 6.) spirituality. Ignoring any of these six elements puts one's life *out of balance.*

The same is true in ministry. The organization cannot focus all its time and resources on "The Calling." Any more than it can spend endless hours getting ready to do ministry but never actually launching.

In the first few months of a startup ministry's life, you will spend most of your time on the foundational tasks covered in **Starting A Ministry**: developing the vision, mission, and purpose, conducting market research, establishing legitimacy, and starting to approach donors and raise funds.

The ministry's Balance Chart might look like this:

Starting A Ministry

60% of the effort is being expended on operations, while fundraising and "The Calling" each receive 20% of the available time.

As the operation's items fall into place, the organization can focus more on fundraising and "The Calling."

Now, a few months later in the life of the ministry, the Balance Chart takes on a new look:

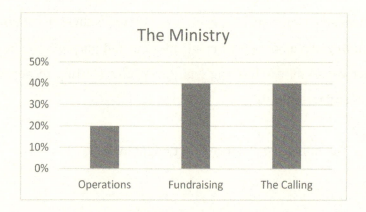

The ministry spends less time on the operations side of the ministry and more hours on fundraising and the actual work on the ground.

Still, more time passes; let's say the timeframe is now 6 to 9 months from launching. Now, suppose we examine the chart:

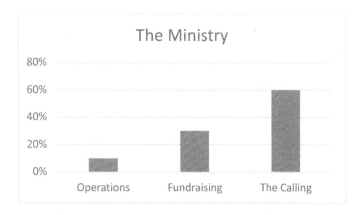

Not all ministries will agree with these simple representations of what items should be worked on for how long.

Some organizations will want to spend more time on the front end, while others feel 30% is insufficient time to fundraise.

These charts only illustrate that each organization must decide how much time they can spend on each activity.

One thing is sure—the ministry must spend time on administration, management, branding, marketing, communications, engagement, fundraising, and donor relations.

 The longer something goes ignored, the more energy it takes to make it right.

Make your best guess on how much time you'll devote to each item and adjust things as time passes.

— 2 —

Calling:
What's Your Why?

What You'll Learn:

- **Learn** to understand your S.H.A.P.E.
- **Learn** to qualify your motivation by answering these four questions.
- **Learn** to use Pastor Rick Warren's seven ways to test whether an impression is from God.

What is your calling? What problem are you interested in solving? What is it you want to make better? How large of an impact do you want to make? How do you transform your vision and passion into positive change?

All good questions.

Passion is essential whether you're starting a ministry or a business.

Passion provides the motivation for finishing well—for finishing at all in some cases, for sticking with it when things get tough, and you feel overwhelmed.

Passion is necessary when developing your message to attract attention, raise awareness, and convert potential donors into committed supporters.

If you're not convinced about your calling, you'll find a helpful list of resources at the end of this chapter to help solidify your decision.

Passion is the bonding agent between a ministry and its supporters, volunteers, staff, and leadership.

It permeates every aspect of an organization, from the conversations between ministry leaders and their supporters to keeping volunteers and staff committed to the vision. It's the linchpin in all the messages that go out on social media, all the stories that get told in the monthly newsletter. It's the key ingredient in the fundraising materials used to garner financial support. The electricity keeps the ministry lights on year after year, obstacle after obstacle, success after success.

Passion is a common thread shared throughout **Starting A Ministry**. In **Chapter 3: Foundational—Turning Your Passion into Purpose**, passion is a key ingredient in forming your Purpose, Vision, and Mission statements. In the Purpose Statement, people must understand your willingness to dedicate time, talent, and resources to solving a daunting problem. In the Vision Statement, passion helps people see the final future result of all the ministry's hard work. In the Mission Statement, they need to know what motivates you to keep going against impossible odds.

In **Chapter 6: Goal Setting—Think Big!** passion converts into objectives. In **Chapter 15: Fundraising—It's Not About the Money,** passion spurs empathy and understanding into commitment and support. In **Chapter 17: Storytelling—Sharing Your Passion** is also fueled with passion.

Passion is not a single individual's feeling but a shared group emotion. In **Chapter 6: Personnel—Readying the Team**, passion is probably the most significant ingredient that should determine the selection of leaders, board members, staff, and volunteers. Misaligned passions lead to unequal motives. Unequal motives lead to disharmony and, perhaps much worse failure.

Passion is sprinkled elsewhere throughout Starting A Ministry; keep your eyes open.

Is Your Passion Calling You?

An endless array of resources can help a person find their calling.

Googling "your calling" produces millions of secular and Christian pages. On YouTube.com, you'll find page after page of videos; more than one person can watch in a lifetime. Tutorials, websites, and social media groups saturate the web, all hawking information about defining one's calling. Of course, there are hundreds of books on Amazon.com, with more added as you read this book.

Rick Warren, pastor of Saddleback Church, did a tremendous six-part series titled "Live Your Calling."

If you're unsure how your calling relates to your spiritual gifts, browse for that information. You'll find plenty of websites offering free spiritual gift tests. Perhaps the church you attend has a spiritual gifts class.

There are also websites hosting S.H.A.P.E. quizzes to help you

Starting A Ministry

discover God's purpose for your life. S.H.A.P.E. stands for Spiritual Gifts, Heart, Abilities, Personality, and Experiences.

Here are four questions people should ask themselves when contemplating a career move:

1. What am I good at?
2. What do I enjoy doing?
3. What do I not do well?
4. What do I hate doing?

God will not call a person to a venture opposed to who they are, what they know, what they've accomplished in life, and what they're talented at doing. That doesn't make sense.

Here's a final set of questions to consider:

- "What will you do if you fail?"
- What if starting a ministry is too hard?
- What if you feel unprepared for the challenge?
- What if the financial support never shows up?
- What if family and friends think you're on the wrong track?
- Will you go back to the job you left?
- Will you try something else?

- Will you retire early?

There is no 5-step, bullet-proof plan that answers these questions.

If unsure, pray, ask God for guidance, and seek counsel from trusted, Godly friends.

There's another good sermon by Rick Warren on YouTube.com titled Learn How to Recognize God's Voice. He talked about seven ways to test an impression we believe is from God:

1. ***Does it agree with the Bible?*** – God doesn't change His mind. He doesn't say one thing and then tell a person something else.

2. ***Does it make me more like Christ?*** – Does this idea make me more like Christ? God's purpose in life is to make you more like Christ.

3. ***Does my church family confirm it?*** – Ask other mature believers what they think of the idea.

4. ***Is it consistent with how God has shaped me?*** – God shaped you before you were born. He does not want you to be somebody you're not.

5. **Does it concern my responsibility?** – Is God talking to you or are you listening for someone else? Everyone has direct access to God. He really does not need to go through you.

6. **Is it convicting rather than condemning?** – Conviction comes from God to correct us. Condemnation comes from Satan to confuse us.

7. **Do I sense God's peace about it?** – If you feel pressure, overwhelmed, or confused about your decision, you're likely caught up in yourself and it's not God's voice. God is not the author of confusion.

The Four Question Worksheet

The Four Question Worksheet

Use this worksheet to work through those four career questions.

1. What are you good at?

   _____
   _____
   _____
   _____

2. What do you enjoy doing?

   _____
   _____
   _____
   _____

3. What do you not do well?

   _____
   _____
   _____
   _____

4. What do you hate doing?

   _____
   _____
   _____
   _____

Copyright © 2019 ministryTHRIVE

The Seven Question Worksheet (1)

The Seven Question Worksheet

Use this worksheet to work through Rick Warrens seven questions on how to recognize God's voice.

1. Does it agree with the Bible?

   _____
   _____
   _____
   _____

2. Does it make me more like Christ?

   _____
   _____
   _____
   _____

3. Does my church family confirm it?

   _____
   _____
   _____
   _____

4. Is it consistent with how God has shaped me?

   _____
   _____
   _____
   _____

Copyright © 2019 ministryTHRIVE

The Seven Question Worksheet (2)

The Seven Question Worksheet
(Part II)

5. Does it concern my responsibility?

   _____
   _____
   _____
   _____

6. Is it convicting rather than condemning?

   _____
   _____
   _____
   _____

7. Do I sense God's Peace about it?

   _____
   _____
   _____
   _____

Copyright © 2019 ministryTHRIVE

− 3 −

Foundational:
Turning Your Passion into Purpose

What You'll Learn:

- **Learn** to build a Statement of Purpose that tells why the organization exists and how it plans to make a difference.
- **Learn** to create a Vision Statement that describes the ministry's destination somewhere in the future.
- **Learn** to develop a Mission Statement that speaks of how the organization plans to achieve its goals. Some would say the mission is the vision in action.

Over the years, people have confused and misused these three assertions: Purpose, Mission, and Vision.

People are unsure of which to use and when.

But let us not concern ourselves with other people's misuse of these statements. Let us ensure we understand what each means and be able to explain and use them with our donors, supporters, and the people we meet.

Here's an easy way to remember which term means what:

The Statement of Purpose – is why the organization has decided to make a difference.

The Mission Statement – is the path the organization sets to reach its goals. Some would say your mission is your vision in action.

The Vision Statement – is your final destination somewhere in the future.

Suppose we create a fictitious organization to experiment with as we develop our sample Statement of Purpose, Mission, and Vision Statements.

In its simplest form, the Statement of Purpose answers four questions:

1. **Why is this needed?** What is the problem or need, and why must it be addressed?

Starting A Ministry

2. **Why this way?** What vital solution(s) (products or services) do we plan to offer to meet the need?

3. **Why us?** Why are we *uniquely* qualified to meet the need?

4. **Why now?** What is the urgency of solving the problem now?

Let us answer these four questions for our fictional organization – Project ANYWHERE.

Why is this needed? Even though the abortion rate in the US fell by 24% between 2006 and 2015, doctors still denied life to 638,169 babies. The Constitution of the United States guarantees everyone *life, liberty, and the pursuit of happiness.* God says, "Each life is of value" and "Taking innocent life is murder." We need alternatives to abortion.

Why this way? Project ANYWHERE plans to open a pregnancy resource center in a well-positioned, fast-growing area in northern Illinois. The PRC will provide counseling, free pregnancy tests, STD screening, and free ultrasound. Free counseling Dos and Don'ts for expecting dads is also available. 64% of post-abortive women say they felt pressured by others to abort.

Why us? Over the past five years, Project ANYWHERE has successfully established two other pregnancy resource centers in nearby towns. Over 1,100 moms opted not to terminate their pregnancy. Four hundred fifty dads attended the Dos and Don'ts training. Nine hundred eighty moms received counseling. Over 1,500 attended the after-abortion risk avoidance training.

> **Why now?** One life lost to abortion is ONE too many. PRCs hand down a legacy of love and protecting the unborn. They also assist moms and dads facing some of life's most difficult decisions. Unchecked, abortive services will continue to take the lives of the unborn in the millions

 Add whatever level of complexity is necessary to explain the organization's purpose clearly and succinctly.

The **Mission** and **Vision Statements** should be brief and to the point.

Mission Statement: Your mission statement should be able to be condensed down to a slogan, a hashtag, or key phrase. Nine words or less, if possible, that identify and symbolize who you are and state your objective – this is your mission statement. "To boldly go where no man has gone before!" Coupled with your project name, this will make your organization memorable. An excellent descriptive mission statement makes people want to learn more about your ministry and what you do.

Mission Statement Examples:

New Horizons Foundation – "Taking your vision to the world."

ProjectCaleb – "Coaching charitable nonprofits to succeed."

Wounded Warrior Project – "To honor and empower wounded warriors."

Whispering Eagle Ministries – "Bringing hope to orphaned children in the Congo."

Vision Statement: If your organization was functioning at its highest capacity, what would it look like? Put another way, "What do you see when you close your eyes and dream about what could be the impact?" What do you want to be "known for" when people think about your ministry? This is what gets you up in the morning!

Vision Statement Examples:

Feeding America – "A hunger-free America."

Habitat for Humanity – "A world where everyone has a decent place to live."

Make-A-Wish – "Our vision is that people everywhere will share the power of a wish."

In Touch Ministries – "Proclaiming the Gospel of Jesus Christ to people in every country of the world."

If the Mission and Vision statements are not memorable, they will not be repeatable.

A Mission Statement Writing Workshop

Writing a Vision, Mission, or Purpose Statement will not happen in one sitting. Developing each statement takes a good deal of thought.

I'll use ministryTHRIVE as my non-profit example for the Vision, Mission, and Purpose statements:

Here's how to develop the Mission Statement:

1. Start by writing down some general thoughts: What will the ministry do, for who, and why? Mission Statements also need to be measurable. Federal Express's mission, "*When you absolutely, positively need it delivered overnight,*" was easy to measure. Either the package arrived safely the next day, or it didn't.

2. Here are some example iterations as the mission statement comes together:

Starting A Ministry

- Provide learning experiences to ministries and nonprofits that enable them to be more effective, efficient, and sustaining. (17 words)
- Provide learning experiences, making ministries more effective, efficient, and sustainable. (13 words)
- Provide world-class learning experiences that will allow ministries to be sustainable. (11 words)
- Coaching ministries to succeed. (4 words)
- Provide learning experiences for Christian ministries and nonprofits. (8 words)
- Learning experiences that enable ministries to thrive. (7 words)
- Learning Experiences = Thriving Ministries. (4 words)
- Helping ministries thrive. (3 words)
- Provide exceptional learning experiences, ensuring ministries thrive. (7 words)

The final version might look like this: "*Providing exceptional learning experiences to those in ministry to ensure they master the skills necessary to achieve their goals.*" (19 words) It's a little long but tells the story. What the ministry does: "*Provide exceptional learning experiences.*" Learning experiences include books, webinars, podcasts, blog articles, presentations, and coaching. To whom: "Those in ministry." Why: "to ensure they master the skills necessary to achieve their goals." Helping others determines the ministry's success.

34 *Turning Your Passion into Purpose*

People's acceptance and success will measure the learning materials we create and deliver.

A Final Examine

Here are two tests to contemplate for the Vision, Mission, and Purpose Statements once they're written: First, if people in the organization cannot remember the mission statement, for instance, when they speak to people, the statement needs adjusting. Second, it needs reworking if potential supporters do not understand what you do after telling them your mission.

Statement of Purpose Worksheet

Statement of Purpose Worksheet

Develop your ministry's Statement of Purpose. Be specific. Try to avoid "church speak."

1. What is the problem or need and why does it need to be addressed?

   _____
   _____
   _____
   _____

2. What vital services do we offer to meet the need?

   _____
   _____
   _____
   _____

3. Why are we *uniquely* qualified to meet the need?

   _____
   _____
   _____
   _____

4. What is the urgency to respond and what will be done with their support?

   _____
   _____
   _____
   _____

Copyright © 2019 ministryTHRIVE

Vision Statement Worksheet

Vision Statement Worksheet

If your organization were functioning at its highest capacity, what would it look like? To put it another way, "what do you see when you close your eyes and dream about what could be the impact of your project". What do you want to be "known for" when people think about your project? This is what gets you up in the morning!

1. Vision 1.0 (4 to 12 words)

   _____
   _____
   _____

2. Vision 2.0 (4 to 12 words)

   _____
   _____
   _____

3. Vision 3.0 (4 to 12 words)

   _____
   _____
   _____

4. Vision 4.0 (4 to 12 words)

   _____
   _____
   _____

Copyright © 2019 ministryTHRIVE

Starting A Ministry

Mission Statement Worksheet (1)

Mission Statement Worksheet

Your Mission Statement should be able to be condensed down to a slogan, a hashtag or key phrase, nine words or less, that identify and symbolize who you are and simply states your objective – this is your Mission Statement. "To boldly go where no man has gone before!"

1. Mission (9 words or less)
   _____
   _____

2. Mission (9 words or less)
   _____
   _____

3. Mission (9 words or less)
   _____
   _____

4. Mission (9words or less)
   _____
   _____

5. Mission (9words or less)
   _____
   _____

6. Mission (9words or less)
   _____
   _____

Copyright © 2019 ministryTHRIVE

Mission Statement Worksheet (2)

Mission Statement Worksheet (2)

7. Mission (9words or less)
   _____
   _____

8. Mission (9words or less)
   _____
   _____

9. Mission (9words or less)
   _____
   _____

10. Mission (9words or less)
    _____
    _____

Copyright © 2019 ministryTHRIVE

— 4 —

Market Research: Doing Your Homework

What You'll Learn:

- **Learn** how to tell what other non-profits are in the area and how they approach the problem the ministry wants to solve.
- **Learn** how to understand better the clients—those being ministered to.
- **Learn** how to test the need and delivery of the proposed product or service.

I Is there a *bona fide* need? Is another nonprofit, for-profit, or government entity already doing the same or similar work or providing a comparable product or service?

Have you ever watched a new business open in town, say a new burger joint, even though McDonald's, Burger King, Wendy's, and Sonic have been well-established in town for years? Soon after the months of extensive remodeling ended, the new business opened to loud fanfare and quietly shut its doors a few months later.

The business' demise might well have been a victim of poor market research.

 God will not call us to fail.

But He will expect us to do our homework.

Market research helps a budding organization:

1. Gain knowledge about who else is in the area and how they approach the problem the ministry wants to solve.
2. Better understand the clients—those being ministered to.
3. Test the need and delivery of the proposed product or service.

 Don't presume to know what people need without asking them first.

Suppose we want to help provide Christian housing for single moms in Colorado Springs, Colorado. Our idea is to solicit grants and donations to acquire rental properties in the most disadvantaged zip codes within the city.

First, we need to understand how many organizations offer similar services to single moms in Colorado Springs.

Who's Ministering in the Area?

A quick scan of the Housing Resources available on the city website informs us there are five: Bloom Recovery Home, Catholic Charities Family Services, Family Life Services, Gospel Homes for Women, and Mary's Home.

Now that we know who's in town, the next logical step would be determining what services each organization offers moms.

Think of building a spreadsheet listing the various services offered by each organization. Once listed, we can look for gaps in available services. Those gaps could well be our niches.

To help you get started, we've looked at five organizations in Colorado Springs and built an example EXCEL spreadsheet.

	A
1	**Bloom Recovery Home**
2	Harbor House Clinic
3	Housing First & Veteran Specific Housing
4	Harbor House Residential
5	Project Harbor
6	Bloom Recovery Home
7	
8	**Catholic Charities Family Services**
9	Family Services
10	Paths to Opportunity
11	Emergency/Essential Services
12	Health & Well-Being
13	
14	**Family Life Services**
15	Transitional Housing
16	Secure Play Areas
17	Mentoring
18	Support Groups
19	Networking Assistance
20	Life Skills Classes
21	Youth Summer Camps
22	
23	**Gospel Homes for Women**
24	Detoxification
25	Therapeutic Intervention
26	Life-Skills Development
27	Relapse Prevention
28	
29	**Mary's Home**
30	Shelter
31	Medical & Behavioral Health Services
32	Life Skills
33	

In our spreadsheet example, we can see that some of the organizations offer similar yet varied services. We'll have to dig deeper to understand how the services differ and where we might fit in or complement the already provided services.

Understanding the Client

Because there is now a spreadsheet, the names of organizations that connect with moms in town are known. The moms could be interviewed to see how the ministry might help.

Based on those results, programs could be aligned to meet the single mom in the community.

Testing the Need

Develop test programs to see if there is interest in the services the ministry proposes.

Perhaps life skill classes could be offered. Or help could be given to single moms with job placement or career advancement.

As a side note, now that you know about the other organizations in the area, are there ones with whom you can form a strategic relationship and who are like-minded? There's strength in numbers.

How to Know If We've Done Our Homework

Answer this short list of questions related to *Doing Your Homework*. On a scale of 1 to 5...

1. Does the organization understand the entities in town that offer the same or similar products or services?

    No 1. ☐ 2. ☐ 3. ☐ 4. ☐ 5. ☐ **Yes**

2. Does the organization understand the people they intend to serve?

    No 1. ☐ 2. ☐ 3. ☐ 4. ☐ 5. ☐ **Yes**

3. Were prototypes and test programs developed to ensure the organization is on the right track in what it plans to offer?

    No 1. ☐ 2. ☐ 3. ☐ 4. ☐ 5. ☐ **Yes**

4. Did the test results confirm the need for the proposed products or services?

No 1. ☐ 2. ☐ 3. ☐ 4. ☐ 5. ☐ **Yes**

If your answers were on the low side of the scale, you may want to consider more testing or delivering different services.

Doing Your Homework Worksheet

Doing Your Homework Worksheet

Answer this short list of questions related to, *Doing Your Homework*. On a scale of 1 to 5...

1. Does the organization understand the entities in town that offer the same or similar products or services?

    No 1. ☐ 2. ☐ 3. ☐ 4. ☐ 5. ☐ Yes

2. Does the organization understand the people they intend to serve?

    No 1. ☐ 2. ☐ 3. ☐ 4. ☐ 5. ☐ Yes

3. Were prototypes and test programs developed to ensure the organization is on the right track in what it plans to offer?

    No 1. ☐ 2. ☐ 3. ☐ 4. ☐ 5. ☐ Yes

4. Did the test results confirm the need for the proposed products or services?

    No 1. ☐ 2. ☐ 3. ☐ 4. ☐ 5. ☐ Yes

If your answers were on the low side of the scales, you may want to consider back-tracking on the items that were lacking.

Copyright © 2019 ministryTHRIVE

— 5 —

Compliance:
Getting Legit, Staying Legit

What You'll Learn:

- **Learn** the difference between filing as a 501(c)(3) and fiscal sponsor.

Forming a corporation like a nonprofit or Charitable C Corp takes roughly seven steps depending on the different regulations within each state. This discussion does not include entities formed outside of the US.

Forming a Legal Entity

The process might look like this:

- **Choosing a name for the organization** – The name chosen must tell people what you do. If something vague is selected, it may make the marketing more difficult. "Corporation," "Incorporated," or "LLC." must follow the name. The Secretary of State's office will tell you if the name is available.

- **Develop and file the articles of incorporation** – The articles usually include the name and address of the organization along with the basic structural information such as the registered agent, membership make-up, and the tax-exempt purpose of the entity. Check out nolo.com for examples.

- **Apply for your IRS and state tax exemptions** – On the federal side, you must request and file an IRS Packet 1023 or 1023-EZ. Some states have differing requirements, so check with the individual state taxing agencies.

- **Draft the bylaws** – These are the nuts and bolts of the organization's operations. For instance, the bylaws would describe how many board members constitute a quorum, how many terms a board member can serve, or electing new members. Check out nolo.com for examples.

 Refrain from all political activities.

- **Choose directors** – Directors or an advisory team provide an excellent sounding board. They provide support, counsel, direction, and accountability and help distill good ideas into great ones. **Chapter 6: Personnel—Readying the Team covers choosing the best candidates for the board.**

- **Hold your first board meeting** – Grab a copy of *Robert's Rules of Order* from Amazon.com. It talks about the structure and operation of a typical board. **Chapter 6: Personnel—Readying the Team also covers this entry in more detail.**

- **Obtain the required licenses and permits** – Check with your state Department of Consumer Affairs to ensure you operate within the law. For instance, you'll need a sales tax permit if you sell anything to consumers.

If you're unsure about anything, consult an attorney.

Choosing a Fiscal Sponsor

 Some organizations opt to go with a fiscal sponsor and not file for 501(c)(3) status at first.

A fiscal sponsor is a nonprofit organization that provides fiduciary oversight, fiscal management, and other services to projects that lack tax-exempt status. This arrangement allows an organization to seek grants and solicit tax-deductible donations under the fiscal sponsor's exempt status. Fiscal sponsors usually charge a fee of between 5 and 15% of the donations for their services. Fiscal sponsors help organizations stay compliant.

Check out these websites:

> www.fiscalsponsordirectory.org
> www.councilofnonprofits.org
> www.fiscalsponsors.org

Partnering May Make Sense

Your calling may not include starting, running, and leading a nonprofit. You may be gifted to work with people experiencing poverty, evangelize, or work with your hands. Running a ministry takes time away from the actual work on the ground. The administration and management are necessary to get the ministry up and running. There's the branding and marketing needed to position the organization properly. Then there's the communication and engagement one must handle to establish relationships with potential donors, and finally, the fundraising and donor relations portion needed to bring in the donations.

 Take time to pray, seek counsel, and weigh your options for starting a ministry from scratch before jumping in.

Protecting the Leadership

Directors and Officer's liability Insurance (often called "D&O") provides coverage for directors and officers of a company. It indemnifies them or the organization for losses or covers defense costs. This insurance applies when a legal action is brought against them for alleged wrongful acts in their official capacities.

Such coverage can extend to defense costs arising out of criminal and regulatory investigations/trials; in fact, civil and criminal actions are often brought against directors/officers simultaneously.

Intentional illegal acts, however, are typically not covered under D&O policies. (Courtesy of Wikipedia.org)

— 6 —

Personnel: Readying the Team

What You'll Learn:

- **Learn** why volunteers give of their time and talents.
- **Learn** how to develop a staffing plan when the desire is to hire an invaluable staff.
- **Learn** the seven secrets to forming a board that will refuse to fail.
- **Learn** the ten ingredients that every good leader possesses.

Jim Collins wrote a terrific book in 2001 titled Good to Great. It's still relevant today. In Good to Great, Jim talks about getting the right people in the right seats on the bus. Having the best people in positions where they can contribute at a high level may determine the organization's success.

 It's tempting to work with family and friends. One might be thinking "cheap labor" can keep expenses down.

 It's hard to fire volunteers. It's even more uncomfortable to let family members go.

Attracting First-class Volunteers

Utilizing volunteer talents and time is paramount to your organization's success if your business is not-for-profit. Getting people to pitch in is not as simple as asking them to help. A successful volunteer strategy takes planning, preparation, time, resources, staff participation, and sound implementation. Success does not come to organizations because they fight for a worthy cause. Assuming we have a mini-planning session and see if we can create a strategy to garner the volunteers the organization so desperately depends upon.

Any basic volunteer strategy will most likely include these essentials:

1. Engaging volunteers.
2. Including volunteers in the organization.
3. Identifying why volunteers offer their time and talents.

4. Keeping volunteers informed and productive.
5. Selecting and recruiting volunteers.
6. Keeping volunteers interested.

Of course, creating a volunteer strategy that works for your organization may have different prerequisites that need investigation and answers. Suppose we look broadly at each of these fundamental components of a volunteer strategy.

Engaging volunteers – there are many good reasons why it makes sense to include volunteers in your organization:

1. To lower expenses.
2. As a means of introducing groups and individuals to your mission.
3. So as not to divert paid-staff resources.
4. To teach children to give to their community, church, or school

 "Because we need your help" is a short-sighted motivation and will not attract many participants.

Include volunteers in the association – ensure the paid staff supports using volunteer help. Otherwise, the paid staff may feel offended, and volunteers may feel like outsiders. To use volunteers best as a resource, the paid staff should actively look for volunteer help. From the volunteer's perspective, they must feel their contribution is necessary and valuable. Volunteers will stay with an effort if they feel fulfilled.

When planning the week's schedule or looking forward to having larger projects done, consider what role volunteers help can play. Many people who volunteer their time would be as glad to donate their skills or talents as their hands and back.

Identifying why volunteers offer their time and talents – seems like a simple statement at first, but it is more complex than it appears. Better stated, it might read, "Understand why people who volunteer their time would want to spend it with *your* ministry?" Here are eight common reasons why people donate their time and talents:

- To gain skills and experience.
- To make new friends.
- To work in the community.
- To meet new people.
- To provide service.
- To gain status.
- To fill time.
- To get out of the house.

Of course, we can devise a list of more altruistic reasons, but why people volunteer at all means very little to your venture. You must uncover why people want to participate in *your* organization's activities.

As we noted last time, volunteers are a fundamental part of any nonprofit organization and are vital to its success. Attracting volunteers to your organization, helping the staff understand the role volunteers play, and identifying why people want to give their time and talents to your group are all essential to a venture's success.

However, keeping volunteers informed and productive, selecting and recruiting volunteers, and keeping volunteers interested over time are also key components.

Keeping volunteers informed and productive – might be seen as two distinct issues facing an organization. People achieve productivity when they pay attention to preparation and the right amount of supervision. *Informed* are what volunteers are not. Somehow, an organization concludes that putting people to work shoveling coal as soon as possible is more valuable than telling them where the ship is heading. Suppose a person understands why they are performing a specific task. In that case, they will undoubtedly be able to do a better job.

An organization could use a newsletter to keep volunteers abreast of the current planning and what comes next.

Starting A Ministry

Selecting and recruiting volunteers is sometimes left to an open door. Just because someone walks into the organization does not necessarily mean they are perfect for the task.

Some fundamental guidelines for qualifying volunteers are:

1. Ensure the volunteer process is fair and equal for all those offering their time and talents.
2. If a volunteer cannot perform the necessary task, look for other ways they can help.
3. Document volunteer policies and procedures ahead of time and do not implement them on the fly.
4. The expectations of the organization and volunteers should be clearly stated and understood by both parties.
5. If a volunteer activity is to occur with youngsters, the association must have an explicit policy on vetting. (In other words, what will the investigation process be before the person is allowed to volunteer around children?)

Regarding the recruitment process, these three questions need answering: Who will do the recruitment, an individual or committee? Second, where will the organization gather the necessary volunteers? And finally, how will the volunteers be attracted to the effort?

Volunteers will sign on if they clearly understand why they are needed, what the work involves, and what the benefits are to the organization and the volunteer collectively.

Hiring Invaluable Staff

Hiring friends who are unemployed or people who get excited when they hear your vision may not be the best candidates. Bringing people on that will work for *short rope* (for cheap), as we say here in Colorado, may not work out either.

Staffing is ultimately about bringing the right people on board. People who have shared goals and priorities. People who want to see the vision become a reality.

The perfect staffing plan ensures the correct number of people with the right skills are in the proper positions. With this personnel formula in place, the organization can confidently execute its mission.

Before the organization acquires new hires, perhaps the question is, can we do more with the current staff? This is not to infer the current staff should work longer hours.

Can reshuffling people into different positions solve the staffing need?

Can reallocating responsibilities fix things?

Can training those onboard eliminate the need for new personnel?

Are there things the organization is doing that it is not suited to do?

If "no" answers all of these questions, it's time to develop a staffing plan. A staffing plan is more about scheduling coffee with people or placing ads on job websites.

A simple staff plan has four steps:

1. **Determine your goals** – What problem are we trying to solve by bringing someone new on?

2. **Size up the talent pool** – Is there a good crop of skilled people in the job pool?

3. **Determine the functional needs** – Write a job description.

4. **Create an actionable plan** – The action plan might include these three processes: 1.) Recruitment, 2.) Interview, and 3.) Hiring. Recruitment: Where will one

look for new hire candidates: churches, other nonprofits, other Christian organizations, job boards, college interns, ask around? Interview: Develop the interview questions ahead of time and practice. Hiring: Make sure each party understands the expectations on both sides well.

Choosing the Right Candidates for the Board

Forming an advisory board or team for your organization makes perfect sense. After all, you don't come equipped with all the skills and talents necessary to do everything that needs doing. Even the Lone Ranger had Tonto.

Advisory teams provide an excellent sounding board. They can help distill your *good ideas* into *great ones*. They can provide invaluable counsel and direction and offer the skills and talents you or your working team of volunteers lack.

So, what goes into forming an advisory board? Consider these seven ingredients, and you'll be well on your way to creating a vital component to your organization's success.

1. **Choosing the right members** – don't choose life-long friends who see things your way. Try enlisting people who know you well and others who may be casual

acquaintances. Choose people who have the experience you or your team lack. Choose people who have gifts that you are missing. Ensure every candidate is interested and passionate about what you're trying to accomplish.

2. **Setting Everyone's Expectations** – Review the organization's mission, vision, and case statements at the first meeting to ensure everyone understands your project's direction well. Make sure they understand your organization's goals for the coming year. Let them know whether this engagement will be an advisory team position or a "working" committee. Tell people upfront what you expect them to commit to: a one-year commitment, attending three 90-minute breakfast meetings a year. Will there be homework or things to bring to each meeting? Are you looking for sound counsel and advice? Email the agenda two weeks before each meeting so team members can prepare their thoughts and finish their assignments. Send meeting minutes out the week after the get-together so people can track the discussions.

3. **Define Each Member's Responsibilities** – If the group will be a "working" team, set everyone's expectations by assigning responsibilities and try your best to gauge how much time people need to commit each month. If you

believe titles are necessary, then assign them. Will a group of people be responsible for the technology or fundraising? Or will committees be formed? If so, will board members chair the various committees? Keep the bureaucracy to a minimum. Don't assign titles because one person feels left out. Make sure each member understands and agrees to their assigned duties.

 Missed expectations may cause conflict.

4. **Pick a Convenient Time and Place to Meet** – Choose a meeting place as convenient and neutral as possible. Choose a comfortable room at church (a fireplace would be a great enticement), a shared room at a community center, or even your living room or kitchen table may help inspire conversation. For example, the advisory team might meet three times a year, once in February, May, and October. The timing here is intentional to avoid summer vacations and family holiday get-togethers. Schedule the meetings last 90 minutes – no marathon get-togethers that end up wearing out your team. Keep things business casual. Offer eats and drinks.

5. **Do "the Ask" in Person** – Emails, texts, and phone calls will not be as effective as face-to-face meetings over a cup of coffee. This brief get-together gives you time to explain

your passion and mission. The person listening can see your composure. Some will likely opt in despite being busy once people sense your excitement for the project. Busy people always make the best candidates to get something done. Follow up whether they decide to join or tell you their schedule won't permit it. Thank them for considering the assignment.

6. **Will Board Members Financially Support the Mission** – Some organizations believe those on the advisory committee or board must support the efforts financially. Make this decision before asking people to be involved. It makes sense on several levels to have team members financially engaged in the work. A conversation with a potential donor might get uncomfortable if the team member is not financially supporting the mission. Board members supporting the effort will undoubtedly be more invested in the organization's success. Having the committee members support the vision also causes them to be more involved in what's happening.

7. **Give Each Person a Way Out** – Not everyone will have the necessary bandwidth (the time), even if you ask them to attend a few breakfast meetings yearly. Be gracious enough and provide them an easy out if they cannot commit. Avoid leaning on people to commit. They usually

never make the best volunteers. If your organization or project does not have an advisory team, consider adding this item to your list of goals for this year.

 Keep the number of board members down to a minimum.

Leadership Skills

If we mentioned everyone else in the organization, how about the leader?

As a postscript, here are ten leadership qualities noted by Sarmad Hasan in his article posted at Taskque.com (Comments paraphrased.):

1. **Honesty and Integrity** – How can a leader expect followers to be honest if the one in charge lacks this core value? Leaders succeed when they stick to their beliefs. They fail when integrity is deficient.

2. **Confidence** – Leaders must exhibit confidence in their direction and decisions. Without this quality, those in the organization will be reluctant to follow.

3. **Inspires Others** – John Quincy Adams (our 6th President of the United States) said best: "*If your actions inspire others to dream more, learn more, do more, and become more, you are a leader.*"

4. **Commitment and Passion** – Leaders must be willing to get their hands dirty. If subordinates see a lack of passion from the leader, they may bolt the organization.

 Don't be in a rush to choose the right person to lead.

5. **Good Communicator** – If a leader's words have the power to motivate. If the person cannot communicate, their message may be lost.

6. **Decision-making Capabilities** – Leaders must make the right decisions at the right time. Looking for consensus is not leading. Yes, the leader must check in with the stakeholders. After all, they are the ones who will benefit from the direction.

7. **Accountability** – Holding people accountable for their actions fosters a sense of responsibility.

8. **Delegation and Empowerment** – Don't micromanage, delegate. The leader cannot and should not do everything.

Truly listen to each candidate's words.

9. **Creativity and Innovation** – Steve Jobs said, "*Innovation distinguishes between a leader and a follower.*"

10. **Empathy** – Leaders who show empathy build a stronger connection with their followers.

Volunteer Application Worksheet

Volunteer Application Worksheet   Date: _____

Use this application example as a jump-off point in designing your own questions.

Name: _____

Phone: _____ Email: _____

Church: _____

Why are you interested in volunteering with ANYWHERE Ministry?
_____
_____
_____

What skills do you bring to the table?
_____
_____
_____

Is there a committee that you'd like to serve on?
_____
_____
_____

Do you have any previous volunteer experience? Yes _____ No _____ Explain?
_____
_____
_____

Are you available during the week? Yes _____ No _____ Mornings _____ Afternoons _____

Are you available on weekends? Yes _____ No _____

Copyright © 2019 ministryTHRIVE

Board Member Application Worksheet

Board Member Application Worksheet

Use this application example as a jump-off point in designing your own questions.

Name: _____

Phone: _____ Email: _____

Occupation: _____

Why are you interested in joining ANYWHERE Ministry?
_____
_____
_____

What skills do you bring to the table?
_____
_____
_____

Is there a committee that you'd like to serve on?
_____
_____
_____

Do you have any previous board experience? Yes _____ No _____ Explain?
_____
_____
_____

Can you commit to our monthly meeting schedule? Yes _____ No _____

Can you commit to being on the board for a two-year term? Yes _____ No _____

Copyright © 2019 ministryTHRIVE

Sample Board Meeting Agenda

ANYWHERE:ministry

123 Maple Street ■ Colorado Springs, CO 80905 ■ 719-555-1212 ■ john@yourdomain.com

Date: November 17, 2018

Re: Advisory Board Agenda

7:00 – Open in Prayer

- Read minutes from last meeting
- Read financial report
- Read volunteer report
- Review services
- Need to have a better understanding of the nonprofits in the city

- Early Goals for 2019
    - Develop Tutorials
        - Project Manager Portal
        - New Project Essentials
        - Existing Project Essentials
    - Begin to develop a Workshop Series
        - Fundraising: It's Not About the Money!

Next Meeting: October 18th, Tuesday dinner 6:00 PM @ 123 Maple Street.

Thanks for your participation, prayer, and support.

Look to Him!
John

Sample Board Meeting Minutes

ANYWHERE:ministry

123 Maple Street ■ Colorado Springs, CO 80905 ■ 719-555-1212 ■ john@yourdomain.com

Date: November 17, 2018

Re: Advisory Team Minutes

Attending: John, Kay, Doug, Steve, Dean, and Isam

7:00 – Meeting Started
- Reviewed Minutes from last meeting – no additions
- Reviewed financial report
- Reviewed volunteer report – volunteer recruiting campaign on track
- Reviewed Services
- Identified three like-minded nonprofit organizations in town
- Early Goals for 2019
    - Develop Tutorials
        - Project Manager Portal – on track
        - New Project Essentials – need assistance
        - Existing Project Essentials – on track
    - Begin to develop a Workshop Series
        - Fundraising: It's Not About the Money! – draft due January 15th.

Next Meetings: May 17th, and Oct. 18th. Tuesday dinners 6:00 PM @ 123 Maple Street.

Thanks for your participation, prayer, and support.

Look to Him,
John

– 7 –

Insurance:
Gotcha Covered

What You'll Learn:

- **Learn** how to instill a culture of care in your ministry.

What is D&O (Directors and Officers) insurance, sometimes known as professional liability insurance? This type of insurance covers those individuals for claims made against them while serving as a director or officer on a board.

This insurance serves as indemnification for losses or advancement of defense costs if an insured suffers such a loss due to a legal action brought for alleged wrongful acts.

Starting A Ministry

 Instill a culture of care.

D&O insurance for an organization with no employees is usually around $600. With a few employees, the coverage comes in around $1200 annually for one million dollars in coverage.

The D&O insurance protects the personal assets of the officers and those on the board.

The intent of this chapter is not to advise any organization on whether they need D&O insurance, who they should buy it from, or how much coverage they should purchase.

 Protect your vision.

Consult your attorney regarding securing this form of insurance.

– 8 –

Budgeting:
Counting the Cost

What You'll Learn:

- **Learn** five good reasons why budgets make perfect sense.
- **Learn** the five most common non-profit budget formats.

Budgeting doesn't seem to be everyone's strong suit. Some of us are better at it than others. But if the ministry is to be successful and sustainable—then budgeting is a must.

Find someone on the team who's good at counting the cost.

Budgets can be exhaustive or straightforward. Again, it's yours to decide.

So, why budget?

Budgets keep you out of debt. Budgets help you achieve your goals. Budgets help you spend your money wisely. A budget allows for guilt-free spending. Because you set the money aside ahead of spending it, there's no guilt associated with the purchase.

 Locate an accountant at church if this is your first budget exercise.

Okay, budgeting makes sense for our ministry. How do we get started?

First, let's understand there's more than one kind of budget.

Find examples over at template.net:

Nonprofit Business Plan Budget – for newly formed nonprofits when drafting their business plan.

Nonprofit Development Budget – when a ministry is large enough, the Development Department will likely have its budget.

Nonprofit Fundraising Budget – fundraising activities have associated expenses.

Nonprofit Grant Budget – drafting grant proposals have program expenses.

Nonprofit Project Budget – use this budget to account for every penny spent on projects.

Let's focus on the most common, the *Nonprofit Business Plan Budget*. Head over to template.net for the other examples.

Here's a snapshot from template.net:

S.no.	Description	1	2	3	Difference
	Major				
1	Government Tax				$ -
2	Staff Salaries				$ -
3	Building Maintenance				$ -
4	Staff Development				$ -
5	Staff Bonus				$ -
6	Insurance				$ -
7	Various billings				$ -
8	New Equipment				$ -
9	Marketing Necessities				$ -
	Total Amount	$ -	$ -	$ -	$ -
	Minor				
10	Staff Necessities				$ -
11	Regular Checking				$ -
12	Festival Payments				$ -
13	Staff Gifts				$ -
14	Celebrations				$ -
15	Meeting Needs				$ -
16	Printings				$ -
17	Funds				$ -
18	Contributions				$ -
19	Minor and Major Repairs				$ -
20	Supplies				$ -
21	Non - Working Staff Wages				$ -
	Total Amount	$ -	$ -	$ -	
	Grand Total :	$ -			

Starting A Ministry

Download the budget template in almost any format for $14.99.

Here's a more straightforward example done in WORD:

Operating Project Budget

PROJECT DETAILS

Project Name: Project ANYWHERE
Email: yourname@gmail.com
Budget Year: 2019

EXPENSE DETAILS

Grants:	n/a
Consultant, Contractor:	n/a
Donation, Grant, Honorariums:	n/a
Equipment Purchases:	$4,000
Equipment Rental & Repairs:	$0
Insurance:	n/a
Legal & Accounting:	$300
Miscellaneous:	$2,000
Office Rent:	Temporary space
Office Supplies:	$500
Print & Postage:	$500
Program Support (General Operating Expense):	
Telephone:	$1,200
Travel & Mileage Expense:	$500
Other Expense(s):	
Website s/w and hosting	$300
Other web s/w	$200
Other Expense(s) (Please Describe):	
Total Amount:	$9,500

Don't worry if you don't have exact numbers at the beginning. As expenses start coming in, adjust the numbers. What's important is that you have a starting point from which to work.

 Account for inflation.

If you prefer using an Excel spreadsheet, go ahead.

Now that you're tracking the expenses follow up with donations to ensure the money is always there to pay the bills.

You'll also want to construct or download (template.net) an annual budget template to track expenses for the entire year.

Starting A Ministry

If the ministry fails, chances are the main reason will not be *insufficient funds*.

  If you search the net for "why nonprofits fail," money is hardly listed in the top five or six reasons.

 Circle back once you have the *Nonprofit Business Plan Budget* underway. Don't forget to use the other budget templates to budget for fundraising, projects, branding, marketing, and grant writing.

A Quick Glossary

Before we start this section next, suppose we make sure we're all using the following terms similarly. Yes, the definitions and use of some terms overlap. Branding and Marketing, for example, both talk about messaging—getting the word.

Branding – promoting a particular product or organization employing advertising and distinctive design.

Marketing – the action or business of promoting and selling products or services, including market research and advertising.

Public Relations – building a favorable image for an organization to the public.

Communication – imparting or exchanging of information or news.

Engagement – using strategic, resourceful content to engage people and create meaningful interactions over time.

Development – cultivation strategies that move a person through a series of stages until they decide to donate or not give.

Fundraising – seeking financial support for a charity, cause, or other enterprise.

– 9 –

Branding: Looking Good

What You'll Learn:

- **Learn** how to incorporate the ministry's personality and values in its brand.
- **Learn** the five key elements that define a brand's DNA.
- **Learn** the three questions ministries should contemplate when developing their brand.

Branding has more to do with the look and feel of the ministry's communique and image than how something is transmitted. Your brochure, website, and Facebook page should represent your brand. They should all share common elements: logo, colors, typography, images, tagline, and packaging.

Everyone knows what organizations these brands represent—they're the top three companies in America.

Appearance is Everything

Think of branding as how the ministry appears and sounds to the public.

Here are a few more branding examples: the look and feel of the newsletter that goes out, whether printed or electronic, and the booth and banners at a national conference, along with the fact that everyone on the team appears in khaki pants and red polo shirts.

 Make your brand easy to understand.

Some would say branding also permeates how an organization delivers its service or products, where it hangs out on the web, and the organization's culture.

For our purposes, we'll stick with branding regarding how the ministry presents itself to the public, no matter what form.

Adrian Porter wrote a great post titled, *How to Define the 5 Key Elements of Your Personal Brand DNA*. Here's a summary:

Brand Purpose – Think about "why" you do what you do. Why does the ministry exist? Why does the organization matter? Starbucks is not in the business of selling coffee. They're selling a place away from home or the office—an experience, a community.

Brand Position – Brand position is that unique space you want to occupy in your audience's mind. When they think of *orphans*, they'll think of you. When they think *evangelism*, they'll think of you. When they think of *helping people experiencing homelessness*, they'll think of you.

Here are three questions to contemplate when developing the ministry's brand:

1. In what market is the organization working?
2. Who is the target audience?
3. What sets us apart from the other ministries or nonprofits in the same space?

Brand Promise – What value does the ministry guarantee? Think of Walmart's brand promise, "Save Money. Live Better." Here are a few more examples:

- Focus on the Family – "Helping Families Thrive"
- Spotify – "Music for everyone"
- L.L. Bean – "The outside is inside everything we make."
- REI – "Bringing the outdoors into the retail experience"
- Southwest – "Low fares. Nothing to hide."

The brand promise is what every audience member (potential supporter, donors) expects each time they engage in the ministry.

Brand Personality & Values – If you describe the ministry in human terms, what might they be: exciting, fun, confident, serious, helpful, service-orientated?

What are the ministry's core values?

Brand Expression – This is where the ministry's logo, website, social media pages, colors, and even the organization's name get their time in the spotlight. Audio may also be part of the brand expression.

The job of brand expression is to trigger immediate recognition and recall in the audience members' minds.

 Let the brand tell your story.

So, remember, the brand promise comprises these five elements: Purpose, Position, Promise, Personality & Values, and Expression.

– 10 –

Marketing:
Crafting Your Message

What You'll Learn:

- **Learn** why it's necessary to identify the audience before constructing the message.
- **Learn** the nine most common reasons organizations communicate with their supporters.
- **Learn** why it's vital every message include a call-to-action.

At the beginning of this section, we read that *marketing* is the process one goes through to develop an organization's message. Marketing can be much more, **assuming we** keep things simple.

Starting A Ministry

Before deciding what to say, we need to determine the audience who will hear the message.

Different Messages

One marketing message will not suit all the varied audiences we desire to reach. Think of the audience segments this way:

- We could have a social enterprise running and want to sell more products.
- Perhaps we want to engage new prospective donors.
- Maybe we have a new service to offer, or we're starting work in a new country.
- We may want to increase donor loyalty.
- We could be launching a volunteer drive.
- We may want to encourage word-of-mouth.
- We could be looking to raise public awareness.
- We might be in the throes of starting a fundraising campaign.
- We may want to keep people informed and up to date on what's happening.

As you can see, these marketing messages would all be quite different.

 Don't tell, show.

The message must be reader focused. It must be what the reader is interested in hearing about. The reader is interested in hearing about the organization. However, they are likely more interested in learning about the ministry's impact. How are they making life better? How are they changing a dire situation?

Call-to-action

The last piece of the marketing message concerns what we want the reader to do after they hear from us. It's known as the call-to-action (CTA). Do we want the reader to subscribe to our newsletter and follow us on Facebook, X (Twitter), or Instagram? Do we want them to volunteer or donate to a specific cause? Multiple calls-to-action confuse. Use just one CTA in a marketing piece

 The call to action must be obvious, clear, and concise.

So, to recap, when crafting our message, we need to develop these three elements: who's our audience, what do we want to say that they care about, and what do we want them to do after they read our communique or post?

> **Did you know?**
> **46%** of emails are opened based on the Subject line.

Here's a messaging example related to writing the Subject line for an email campaign. DigitalMarketer.com offers eight forms. The subject line might include self-interest, curiosity, offer, urgency, humanity, news, social proof, and story.

Let's study an example of each:

Self-interest:

Read about how ministryTHRIVE is changing the face of fundraising.

Curiosity:

More non-profits turn to ministryTHRIVE for fundraising help. Why?

Offer:

Attend a FREE ministryTHRIVE workshop at the end of the year
Fundraising.

Urgency:

Tomorrow is the last chance to register for the FREE Fundraising Workshop.

Humanity:

Find out how WeighOut's after-school programs keep youth off the streets and help improve their school grades.

News:

Learn how Ghana is becoming the first developed African country by 2029.

Social Proof:

Find out why the average American spends 5.25 hours each day on their mobile phone.

Social Proof: Social proof is the influence that the actions and attitudes of the people around us (either in real life or online) have on our behavior. The "proof" element is the idea that it must be correct if other people are doing it (or saying it).

Story:

Did Jack really lack the right stuff for his church's mission trip?

 Make sure the call to action is donor focused.

– 11 –

Public Relations:
Being Seen in All the Right Places

What You'll Learn:

- **Learn** eight, no-cost ways to increase the awareness of the ministry's work.
- **Learn** why it's just as essential to measure the effect of the PR as it is to perform the activities.

Public Relations—the building of a favorable image in public. While *marketing* is about driving revenue through messaging, public relations is about the drive to create a positive reputation.

Many would see PR as an integral part of marketing. We've separated it here to clarify its distinct role better.

Raise Awareness

PR's essential role is to get the word out and raise awareness of the ministry.

- The organization may explore opportunities to discuss the ministry's work on local radio and TV stations.

- Perhaps the local newspaper would be willing to do a feature story on the organization's work.

- The ministry could decide to appear at city-wide events to raise its visibility.

- They could speak at churches or other organizational meetings.

- They might offer to write guest posts on influencer blogs.

- Use a social media or email campaign to get the word out.

- The ministry could form strategic relationships with like-minded organizations to increase awareness.

- Send press releases out.

 Know your audience.

Starting A Ministry

Measuring Your Effect

Remember, Public Relations is not fundraising. It's not a good idea to mix the two. Public relations aim to raise the ministry's visibility and awareness. It aims to let people know you're out there and what you're doing. What effect are you having on the problem?

After choosing the PR tactics, measure the efforts. You need to know which ones are working and which ones are not.

PR's job is to generate excitement and interest. Excitement and interest are qualitative and will be hard to measure. The actions that people take can be measured.

You'll have to decide on specific goals and how you want to measure the effectiveness of the public relations campaign. Being able to hand out all 10,000 bottles of water on a hot summer day is a misguided goal. No matter the goals, there must be a call to action. What do you want the people to do after hearing your story? If people are not responding, stop.

Suppose we look at ways to measure the eight bullet items we mentioned under Raise Awareness.

- **Talk on local radio and TV stations** – a radio or TV station may say they have tens of thousands of listeners or viewers. But how many are listening and watching when you're on? Suppose you mentioned your social media handles or told people to visit the website. You could measure that traffic with tools like Facebook's Insights or Google's Analytics. Here, interest is more of a *qualitative* measure. If you offered a copy of your latest book or gave away a free downloadable resource, you could measure people's actions. Actions would be more of a quantitative measurement. People have shown they're more serious about knowing what the ministry is up to. You need a call to action.

 Email the host or producer beforehand so you're prepared for anything.

- **Feature story in a local newspaper** – we could ask the newspaper what their circulation is, but that wouldn't tell us how many people read the feature story about our organization. We'd have to try the same practice of offering something so we can steer people to a landing page and count people's actions. You need a call to action.

- **Appear at city-wide events** – it is a great place to meet and talk with people. If we handed out brochures or stickers with the ministry's website name, we could measure the visitor traffic to see if we notice a bump. You need a call to action.

 Remember, you're not at the event as a spectator.

- **Speak at churches or other organizational meetings** – if attendees ask about volunteering or helping in some other way or if they want to know more about what the ministry is doing, those are all excellent signs speaking at the event was a success. What is the call to action?

- **Write guest posts on influencer blogs** – if readers from the influencer sites start visiting your website, that's good. Now, you need to educate those people until they take action to move the relationship to the next level.

- **Social media or email campaigns** – again, action is everything. Good analytic options and reports exist when using social media or automated email programs such as MailChimp or ConstantContact. Focus on the most meaningful numbers.

- **Form strategic relationships** – you'll have to develop expectations on both sides when forming strategic relationships. What is it you're looking for from each other's audiences?

Make sure the alliance is a two-way street.

- **Press releases** – same applies as when speaking on radio or TV.

Make sure your target audience is listening no matter what the PR tactic. There is nothing to gain from talking to people who have no interest in hearing about the ministry's work.

Public Relations Worksheet (1)

Public Relations Worksheet

Use this worksheet to develop your ideas on raising the awareness of your ministry. Keep in mind, you'll want to measure the effectiveness of whatever tactics you employ.

1. What city-wide events are happening this year?

   _____
   _____
   _____

2. What radio or TV spots would be interested?

   _____
   _____
   _____

3. Can we get the local paper to do a feature story?

   _____
   _____
   _____

4. What strategic alliances could we form with like-minded organizations?

   _____
   _____
   _____

5. What local churches or groups would be up for hearing our message?

   _____
   _____
   _____

Copyright © 2019 ministryTHRIVE

Public Relations Worksheet (2)

6. What influencers (social media, blogs) are our audience reading?
   _____
   _____
   _____

7. _____ (your idea?)
   _____
   _____
   _____

8. _____ (your idea?)
   _____
   _____
   _____

9. _____ (your idea?)
   _____
   _____
   _____

10. _____ (your idea?)
    _____
    _____
    _____

Copyright © 2019 ministryTHRIVE

– 12 –

Communication: Talking the Talk

What You'll Learn:

- **Learn** why listening is just as important as speaking when communicating with supporters.
- **Learn** the seven elements that make up a typical communication plan.
- **Learn** what's involved in building a trouble-free e-mail communication plan.

Think of communication as the tactics used to impart or exchange information. For this discussion, we'll have two elements to work on: how to communicate and when to converse. To answer those two questions, we'll need to develop what's known as a *Communication Plan*.

A Communication Plan

These plans can be simple or quite complex. The plan needs to include the budget, the communication platform, the timing, the subject matter, who's responsible for publishing the communique, and how the metrics will be captured and measured.

Suppose we want to use an email campaign to offer specialized training to volunteers. Here's what the communication plan might resemble:

- Email 1. Sent out upon registering for the free training. This email confirms they've successfully signed up for the training.
- Email 2. Sent out on Day 3. It focuses on a significant benefit to the volunteers that take the training.
- Email 3. Sent out on Day 7. Focuses on a second significant benefit.
- Email 4. Sent out on Day 13. Focuses on what the volunteers will learn.
- Email 5. Sent out on Day 15. It focuses on what the volunteers can do with the learned skill.
- Email 6. Sent out on Day 17. Reminds the volunteers of the start date.

 Communication is more about listening than talking.

Now, let's review the requirements of a typical communication plan.

- Email is a low-cost tactic, that keeps the budget to a minimum.
- The communication platform will be email.
- The timing is sent over 17 days. We must decide on the start date.
- The subject matter is the volunteer training.
- The volunteer coordinator will send out the emails.
- Send the email through an automated service like MailChimp. Gather the metrics and review the reports.
- Now, we can examine how many volunteers opened the email and how many signed up for the training.

You may want the communication plan to be more complex.

Following Up

Suppose we develop a follow-up plan when donors give to the ministry's work. The donors will likely fall into three categories: one-time givers, monthly supporters, and significant donors.

Notice each group is treated differently in this January example.

January		
One-time Gift		Immediate
		Email tax deductible receipt sent by email.
		Within 24 Hours
		Personalized email thanking the person and highlight the gift's impact.
Monthly Gift		Immediate
		Email tax deductible receipt sent by email.
		Within 24 Hours
		Phone call is possible thanking the person and highlight the gift's impact.
Major Donor		Immediate
		Email tax deductible receipt sent by email.
		Within 24 Hours
		Phone call thanking the person and highlight the gift's impact.

In some cases, plan two-way communication.

We'll discuss that subject in **Chapter 13: Engagement—Walking the Walk**.

Sample Communication Plan by Donor Schedule (1)

Sample Communication Plan
By Donor Schedule

Here's what a yearly schedule might look like when communicating with all three donor types. Let's say the three groups all start giving in January.

January
One-time Gift — Immediate
Email tax deductible receipt sent by email.
Within 24 Hours
Personalized email thanking the person and highlight the gift's impact.
Monthly Gift — Immediate
Email tax deductible receipt sent by email.
Within 24 Hours
Phone call is possible thanking the person and highlight the gift's impact.
Major Donor — Immediate
Email tax deductible receipt sent by email.
Within 24 Hours
Phone call thanking the person and highlight the gift's impact.

February
One-time Gift — Personalized email highlighting their gift and the project's impact.
Monthly Gift — Personalized email highlighting their gift and the project's impact.
Major Gift — Phone calls highlighting their gift and the project's impact. Followed up by email with details of the phone call.
Phone call telling another donor's story on how supporting the project is changing their life. Followed up by email with details of the phone call.

March
One-time Gift — Personalized email telling another donor's story on how supporting the project is changing their life. Ask for a second gift.
Monthly Gift — Personalized email telling another donor's story on how supporting the project is changing their life.
Major Gift — Phone calls highlighting their gift and the project's impact. Followed up by email with details of the phone call.
Major Gift — Phone call telling another donor's story on how supporting the project is changing their life. Followed up by email with details of the phone call.

April
Monthly Gift — Personalized email highlighting their gift and the project's impact.
Monthly Gift — Email newsletter recap of past successes and needs.

Copyright © 2019 ministryTHRIVE

Sample Communication Plan by Donor Schedule (2)

Sample Communication Plan
By Donor Schedule

Major Gift	Phone calls highlighting their gift and the project's impact. Followed up by email with details of the phone call. Phone call telling another donor's story on how supporting the project is changing their life. Followed up by email with details of the phone call.
Major Gift	Email newsletter recap of past successes and needs.
May	
Monthly Gift	Personalized email telling another donor's story on how supporting the project is changing their life.
Major Gift	Phone calls highlighting their gift and the project's impact. Followed up by email with details of the phone call. Phone call telling another donor's story on how supporting the project is changing their life. Followed up by email with details of the phone call.
June	
Monthly Gift	Personalized email highlighting their gift and the project's impact.
Major Gift	Phone calls highlighting their gift and the project's impact. Followed up by email with details of the phone call. Phone call telling another donor's story on how supporting the project is changing their life. Followed up by email with details of the phone call.
July	
One-time Gift	Personalized email highlighting project's impact. Email newsletter recap of past successes and needs.
Monthly Gift	Personalized email telling another donor's story on how supporting the project is changing their life.
Monthly Gift	Email newsletter recap of past successes and needs.
Major Gift	Phone calls highlighting their gift and the project's impact. Followed up by email with details of the phone call. Phone call telling another donor's story on how supporting the project is changing their life. Followed up by email with details of the phone call.
Major Gift	Email newsletter recap of past successes and needs.
August	
Monthly Gift	Personalized email highlighting their gift and the project's impact.
Major Gift	Phone calls highlighting their gift and the project's impact. Followed up by email with details of the phone call. Phone call telling another donor's story on how supporting the project is changing their life. Followed up by email with details of the phone call.

Copyright © 2019 ministryTHRIVE

Sample Communication Plan by Donor Schedule (3)

Sample Communication Plan
By Donor Schedule

September
One-time Gift
Monthly Gift   Personalized email telling another donor's story on how supporting the project is changing their life.
Major Gift   Phone calls highlighting their gift and the project's impact. Followed up by email with details of the phone call.
Phone call telling another donor's story on how supporting the project is changing their life. Followed up by email with details of the phone call.

October
One-time Gift   Personalized email highlighting project's impact.
Email newsletter recap of past successes and needs.
Monthly Gift   Personalized email highlighting their gift and the project's impact.
Monthly Gift   Email newsletter recap of past successes and needs.
Major Gift   Phone calls highlighting their gift and the project's impact. Followed up by email with details of the phone call.
Phone call telling another donor's story on how supporting the project is changing their life. Followed up by email with details of the phone call.
Major Gift   Email newsletter recap of past successes and needs.

November
One-time Gift   See Sample EOY Communication Plan Schedule.
Monthly Gift   See Sample EOY Communication Plan Schedule.
Major Gift   See Sample EOY Communication Plan Schedule.

December
One-time Gift   See Sample EOY Communication Plan Schedule.
Monthly Gift   See Sample EOY Communication Plan Schedule.
Major Gift   See Sample EOY Communication Plan Schedule.

Copyright © 2019 ministryTHRIVE

Sample Communication Plan by Channel (1)

Communication Plan by
Channel Example

Make the communication touches brief, concise and to the point. The newsletter should be a page or less. The blog and social media posts should be no more than 25 to 100 words. The Email recap should be short, perhaps a half-page.

January
Newsletter — Week 1 – Highlight project progress, lives being changed, individual's stories
Blog — Weeks 2 and 3 – post what's happening, develop a story line
Social Media — Weekly – one or two posts telling what's happening
Email — Week 4 – Recap newsletter highlights, blog and social media posts
Support Letter — Week 4 – Recap progress made, impact, challenges overcome, obstacles, financial support needed

February
Newsletter — Week 1 – Highlight project progress, lives being changed, individual's stories
Blog — Weeks 2 and 3 – post what's happening, develop a story line
Social Media — Weekly – one or two posts telling what's happening
Email — Week 4 – Recap newsletter highlights, blog and social media posts
Support Letter — Week 4 – Recap progress made, impact, challenges overcome, obstacles, financial support needed

March
Newsletter — Week 1 – Highlight project progress, lives being changed, individual's stories
Blog — Weeks 2 and 3 – post what's happening, develop a story line
Social Media — Weekly – one or two posts telling what's happening
Email — Week 4 – Recap newsletter highlights, blog and social media posts
Support Letter — Week 4 – Recap progress made, impact, challenges overcome, obstacles, financial support needed

April
Newsletter — Week 1 – Highlight project progress, lives being changed, individual's stories
Blog — Weeks 2 and 3 – post what's happening, develop a story line
Social Media — Weekly – one or two posts telling what's happening
Email — Week 4 – Recap newsletter highlights, blog and social media posts
Support Letter — Week 4 – Recap progress made, impact, challenges overcome, obstacles, financial support needed

May
Newsletter — Week 1 – Highlight project progress, lives being changed, individual's stories
Blog — Weeks 2 and 3 – post what's happening, develop a story line
Social Media — Weekly – one or two posts telling what's happening
Email — Week 4 – Recap newsletter highlights, blog and social media posts
Support Letter — Week 4 – Recap progress made, impact, challenges overcome, obstacles, financial support needed

June
Newsletter — Week 1 – Highlight project progress, lives being changed, individual's stories
Blog — Weeks 2 and 3 – post what's happening, develop a story line

Copyright © 2019 ministryTHRIVE

Sample Communication Plan by Channel (2)

Social Media	Weekly – one or two posts telling what's happening
Email	Week 4 – Recap newsletter highlights, blog and social media posts
Support Letter	Week 4 – Recap progress made, impact, challenges overcome, obstacles, financial support needed

July

Newsletter	Week 1 – Highlight project progress, lives being changed, individual's stories
Blog	Weeks 2 and 3 – post what's happening, develop a story line
Social Media	Weekly – one or two posts telling what's happening
Email	Week 4 – Recap newsletter highlights, blog and social media posts
Support letter	Week 4 – Recap progress made, impact, challenges overcome, obstacles, financial support needed

August

Newsletter	Week 1 – Highlight project progress, lives being changed, individual's stories
Blog	Weeks 2 and 3 – post what's happening, develop a story line
Social Media	Weekly – one or two posts telling what's happening
Email	Week 4 – Recap newsletter highlights, blog and social media posts
Support Letter	Week 4 – Recap progress made, impact, challenges overcome, obstacles, financial support needed

September

Newsletter	Week 1 – Highlight project progress, lives being changed, individual's stories
Blog	Weeks 2 and 3 – post what's happening, develop a story line
Social Media	Weekly – one or two posts telling what's happening
Email	Week 4 – Recap newsletter highlights, blog and social media posts
Support Letter	Week 4 – Recap progress made, impact, challenges overcome, obstacles, financial support needed

Suspend regular communication schedule and shift to EOY plan

October

Email	Week 2 – Send out warmup announcement the EOY theme
Blog	Week 3 – Post story about impact made during the year
Social Media	Week 3 – Create Facebook post linking to Donate page

November

Email	Week 1 – Continue to show impact/immediate needs
	Week 1 – Announce GivingTuesday campaign
	Week 3 – Hold GivingTuesday event
	Week 4 – Thank people for participating in GivingTuesday
Blog	Week 2 – Post story about impact made during the year
	Week 3 – Post story about impact made during the year
	Week 3 – Hold GivingTuesday event
	Week 4 – Thank people for participating in GivingTuesday
Social Media	Week 3 – Continue GivingTuesday campaign
	Week 3 – Hold GivingTuesday event
	Week 4 – Thank people for participating in GivingTuesday

Copyright © 2019 ministryTHRIVE

Sample Communication Plan by Channel (3)

December
Email   Week 1 – Send out EOY email talking about successes
                      Week 2 – Send out EOY email asking for donation/talking about needs
                      Week 3 – Send out EOY email asking for donation/ talking about impact
                      Week 4 – Send out "Time is running out" EOY email

Blog   Week 1 – Post story about impact
                      Week 2 – Post story about impact
                      Week 3 – Post story about impact
                      Week 4 – Post story about impact

Social Media   Week 1 – Create Facebook post linking to Donate page
                      Week 2 – Create Facebook post linking to Donate page
                      Week 3 – Create Facebook post linking to Donate page
                      Week 3 – Create Facebook post linking to Donate page

January
Email   Week 1 – Thank donors/talking about successes

Blog   Week 1 – Thank donors/talking about successes

Social Media   Week 1 – Thank donors/talking about successes

Copyright © 2019 ministryTHRIVE

– 13 –

Engagement: Walking the Walk

What You'll Learn:

- **Learn** why it's vital for both parties to act for engagement to survive and flourish.
- **Learn** about the 10 ingredients that guarantee the success of an engagement strategy.
- **Learn** eight simple communication practices to keep donors abreast of what's happening.

Engagement is the participation of someone who shows interest. That means both parties are taking some *action* to move a relationship along.

Sending out emails that never produce a reply is not engagement. Posting articles on a blog that never garners Shares, Likes, or Comments is not engagement. Sending out newsletters that never generate follow-ups by its readers is not engagement.

Engagement Needs Movement

Engagement means both parties are involved in building or strengthening a relationship. If the recipient never acts, there *is* no relationship to foster.

 Always be personable.

If we were to develop an engagement strategy, what might it include?

- What we say must be donor focused.
- The information must be timely.
- What's shared must be attractive.
- Personalize the message.
- Readers must feel they can relate to your brand.
- There must be a positive donor experience.
- Encourage feedback and comments.
- Be sure to share your passion.
- Be authentic.
- Listen, listen, and listen more.

Now that we know what goes into an engagement strategy, how does one put it into play?

Here are some ideas:

- Invite potential supporters and donors to events.
- If you're on social media, answer people's comments in a timely fashion.
- If people Comment, Like, or Share your written post, thank them. Try to start up a conversation. Check out their social pages and comment back.
- Make your followers aware of volunteer opportunities.
- Consider opening opportunities to be on the board on a case-by-case basis.
- Invite them to be a part of the ongoing project.
- Ask people to be a part of a peer-to-peer fundraiser.
- Invite people to subscribe to the ministry's newsletter or blog.

 Be multi-channeled.

Let's assume our organization works in impoverished neighborhoods. We have a weekly Bible study for men and women. We have mentor classes on Wednesday nights and an open gym night for high school students on Tuesday evenings. We do a quarterly men's breakfast at one of the local churches in the neighborhood. We help tutor elementary students who are in danger of being left behind.

The tactics you use (newsletter, email, social media, blog posts) to engage people are up to you.

A simple engagement strategy might look like this:

January – Invite supporters to the men's quarterly breakfast. Inform people about the men's and women's Bible studies.

February – Let people know about the mentoring class and open gym night. Tell people about the successes of the afterschool tutoring program and invite them to volunteer.

March – Inform people about the content of men's and women's Bible studies.

April – Invite supporters to the men's quarterly breakfast.
Let people know about the mentoring class and open gym night. Tell people about the successes of the afterschool tutoring program and invite them to volunteer. Send out a Happy Easter message.

May – Inform people about the content of men's and women's Bible studies. Send out an Enjoy the Summer message.

Starting A Ministry

June – Let people know about the mentoring class and open gym night. Tell people about the successes of the afterschool tutoring program and invite them to volunteer.

July – Invite supporters to the men's quarterly breakfast. Inform people about the content of men's and women's Bible studies.

August – Let people know about the mentoring class and open gym night. Tell people about the successes of the afterschool tutoring program and invite them to volunteer.

September – Inform people about the content of men's and women's Bible studies.

October – Invite supporters to the men's quarterly breakfast. Let people know about the mentoring class and open gym night. Tell people about the successes of the afterschool tutoring program and invite them to volunteer.

November – Inform people about the content of the men's and women's Bible studies. Send out a Happy Thanksgiving message.

December – Let people know about the mentoring class and open gym night. Tell people about the successes of the

Starting A Ministry

afterschool tutoring program and invite them to volunteer. Send out a message celebrating the Birth of Our Savior.

Ensure the messages include a solid call to action if you want the reader to do something. Don't assume people will join, volunteer, or donate.

Of course, your strategy may look quite different from this one.

Engagement Strategy Worksheet (1)

Engagement Strategy Worksheet

Use this worksheet to develop your engagement strategy. Do it for a period of 90 days to see how your ideas work and then expand it.

January

_____
_____
_____

February

_____
_____
_____

March

_____
_____
_____

April

_____
_____
_____

May

_____
_____
_____

Copyright © 2019 ministryTHRIVE

Engagement Strategy Worksheet (2)

June

_____
_____
_____

July

_____
_____
_____

August

_____
_____
_____

September

_____
_____
_____

October

_____
_____
_____

Copyright © 2019 ministryTHRIVE

Engagement Strategy Worksheet (3)

November
_____
_____
_____

December
_____
_____
_____

Copyright © 2019 ministryTHRIVE

– 14 –

Development: Making New Friends

What You'll Learn:

- **Learn** donor relationships are not built overnight. They take time, attention, and patience.
- **Learn** the 12 relationship areas every ministry needs to be proficient in.
- **Learn** why listening may produce better results than speaking.

Development is the art of creating cultivation strategies that move a person through a series of stages until they donate. Development is all about building relationships. Relationships are not built overnight. They take time, energy, and patience.

Relationship Building

Listed here are 12 relationship building areas every organization needs to be proficient in:

Cultivate – Donor relations are not grown overnight. Relationships take time. They take energy. They take effort. Blasting out a generic newsletter to all potential supporters and current donors is not *relationship building*. A gardener does not plant a seed in one minute and expect a flowering plant the next. Think of developing a cultivation plan where the organization maps out its goals and activities to build relationships with its potential supporters and current donors.

 Communicate regularly.

Explain the investment – Donors must understand where their money goes and what its impact is. Don't assume anything. Lay the details out regularly. Be transparent—not vague. Be honest. When progress stalls, tell the donors the plans to turn the situation around.

Understand your donor's passion – There must be an emotional connection between the organization and its donors. It's impossible to get someone excited about the baseball playoffs in the fall if the person has no interest in the game. Passion is the emotional lynchpin that holds the relationship together. Share your passion. Be real.

Treat donors how you want them to treat you – Consider what motivates you to give to a cause and what discourages you. Your donors have similar expectations. Treat donors well, make them feel special, and have them believe they're making a difference. They need to feel confident that supporting your effort was the right choice. Treat every donor as your most important supporter.

Get their attention – Use real people in real situations when telling your stories. Supporters need to see the organization in action. Share passion through pictures and accounts of how the ministry impacts people's lives.

Stay connected – Stay connected with your donor in ways they expect. The younger crowd will be more social-minded, so don't send them printed newsletters and other materials in the US Mail. The more mature supporters might like receiving printed materials. Understand how your donors connect with people and adjust how the organization communicates.

Be responsive – When asked questions, respond in a timely manner. Replying to someone's email when you have time is not necessarily the best gauge of being responsive. Set aside a few times during the day to answer donor questions.

Starting A Ministry

 Be Genuine.

Follow up – Create a tier system of following up with donors. Those who give more financially will expect a more substantial follow-up method. For instance, thank anyone who donates within 24 hours. Those who donate more should receive a handwritten note and a follow-up phone call. Don't treat every donor the same.

Use your database – Your contact information for supporters must reside in a donor management software package, other databases, or an EXCEL spreadsheet. The personal information collected is the lifeblood of the organization when it comes to building relationships.

 "Everyone in the organization is on the Development Team."

Ensure everyone in the organization, board members, staff, and volunteers, understands that building relationships is an all-hands-on-deck effort.

Enjoy building relationships with donors or get someone who does – Donors can spot insincerity from miles away. Building relationships will be nearly impossible if your heart is not in the process. Learn how to enjoy the process or replace yourself.

Different people will want varying degrees of a relationship – Major donors and regular supporters will desire more of a relationship than someone who donates once. Create a tier system to stay in touch with donors. Email some. Call some. And have coffee or lunch with the donors who show the most interest.

Listen, listen, listen – This area may be listed last, but it's undoubtedly the most important. If you're not listening, you won't learn what the donor believes is most important. Stop talking about the organization. Stop talking about *your* dreams. How will we understand what our donors need and want if we're not listening? People get more excited talking about their passion, not by listening to someone else dialog about theirs.

As an unexpected bonus, you'll find out that relationship building leads to increased donor retention and a higher degree of gift giving.

How about taking a short quiz on the 12 relationship building areas to see how your ministry is doing?

Relationship Building Quiz (1)

Relationship Building Quiz

Take a minute or two to grade your ministry on how well it's doing building relationships with potential supporters and donors. On a scale of 1 to 5...

1. *Cultivate* – Donor relations are not grown overnight. Relationships take time. They take energy. They take effort.

    Not So Great 1. ☐ 2. ☐ 3. ☐ 4. ☐ 5. ☐ Great

2. *Explain the investment* – It's important for donors to understand how, where and, why their money is being spent and the impact that is being derived as a result of the organization's efforts.

    Not So Great 1. ☐ 2. ☐ 3. ☐ 4. ☐ 5. ☐ Great

3. *Understand your donor's passion* – There needs to be an emotional connect between the organization and its donors.

    Not So Great 1. ☐ 2. ☐ 3. ☐ 4. ☐ 5. ☐ Great

4. *Treat donors the way you want to be treated* – Think about what makes you give to a cause and what makes you stop giving. Your donors are not any different.

    Not So Great 1. ☐ 2. ☐ 3. ☐ 4. ☐ 5. ☐ Great

5. *Get their attention* – Use real people in real situations when telling your stories. It's important for supporters to see the organization in action.

    Not So Great 1. ☐ 2. ☐ 3. ☐ 4. ☐ 5. ☐ Great

6. *Stay connected* – Stay connected the way your donor expects and prefer.

    Not So Great 1. ☐ 2. ☐ 3. ☐ 4. ☐ 5. ☐ Great

Copyright © 2019 ministryTHRIVE

Relationship Building Quiz (2)

7. **Be responsive** – When asked questions, respond in a timely manner.

    Not So Great 1. ☐ 2. ☐ 3. ☐ 4. ☐ 5. ☐ Great

8. **Follow up** – Create a tiered system of following up with donors.

    Not So Great 1. ☐ 2. ☐ 3. ☐ 4. ☐ 5. ☐ Great

9. **Use your database** – It's vital your contact information for supporters reside in a donor management software package, other database, or an EXCEL spreadsheet.

    Not So Great 1. ☐ 2. ☐ 3. ☐ 4. ☐ 5. ☐ Great

10. **Enjoy building relationships with donors or get someone who does** – Insincerity can be spotted from miles away.

    Not So Great 1. ☐ 2. ☐ 3. ☐ 4. ☐ 5. ☐ Great

11. **Different people will want different degrees of a relationship** – Major donors and regular supporters will desire more of a relationship than perhaps someone who donates once.

    Not So Great 1. ☐ 2. ☐ 3. ☐ 4. ☐ 5. ☐ Great

12. **Listen, listen, listen** – This area may be listed last, but it's undoubtedly the most important. If you're not listening, you won't learn what the donor feels is most important.

    Not So Great 1. ☐ 2. ☐ 3. ☐ 4. ☐ 5. ☐ Great

If you scored more on the "Not So Great" side, it's time to reexamine your relationship building strategy.

Copyright © 2019 ministryTHRIVE

– 15 –

Fundraising:
It's Not About the Money

What You'll Learn:

- **Learn** the chief difference between fundraising and fundraisers.
- **Learn** about the ten most common ways to raise funds and decide which may work best for your ministry.
- **Learn** about the frequent fundraising failures and keep your distance.

This chapter does not cover all the ins and outs of the fundraising process. To do fundraising justice, an entire book of its own is required. This author wrote two books on fundraising titled ***Ignite Your Fundraising*** and ***Ignite Your End-of-the-year Fundraising,*** both of which are available on Amazon.com.

Suppose we make sure we're using the same terminology as we start this chapter. A *fundraiser* is an event, such as a walk-a-thon, silent auction, or bake sale. *Fundraising* is a process—a year-long, never-ending, all-hands-on-deck effort.

Where Will the Revenue Come From?

There are a variety of ways to generate revenue:

- Hold special events or annual dinners.
- Seek funds from businesses or organizations.
- Pursue grants.
- Organize: 5K or 10K runs, bake sales, raffles, silent auctions, car smashing, etc.
- Initiate matching gift drives.
- Encourage peer-to-peer fundraising.
- Look into estate planning.
- Enlist GoFundMe campaigns.
- Open an online store.
- Start a social enterprise.

The organization must decide how to generate the necessary funds so the ministry can achieve its goals.

Fundraising Fails

Before you examine how organizations run successful fundraising campaigns, take a few minutes to note the most common fundraising failures to avoid:

- Failure in **Choosing the Best Time**.
- Failure in **Creating a Clear, Concise Message**.
- Failure in **Explaining the Mission**.
- Failure in **Letting People Know Who You Are**.
- Failure to **Have a Written Plan**.
- Failure to **See the Fundraising Effort as a Priority**.
- Failure in **Thinking Too Small**.
- Failure to **Reach the Right Audience**.
- Failure to **Use the Best Tactics**.
- Failure to **Innovate**.
- Failing to **Make the Call-to-action**.
- Failure to **Pay Attention to Details**.
- Failure to **Create Specific, Measurable, Attainable, Relevant, and Time-bound Goals**.
- Failure to **Pick the Right Person for the Right Job**.
- Failure to **Lead**.

You may be able to add a few more bullets to this list.

As you can see, fundraising efforts can fail for various reasons besides not generating the necessary funds. The fundraising goals may have been unrealistic. Perhaps fundraisers chose the wrong tactics, or they created weak or non-existent calls to action. Poor leadership may have even been a contributing factor.

Build strategies once the organization decides which funding avenues to explore.

Fundraising plans aren't much different than any other strategy. A typical plan includes goals, metrics, audience, message, people, strategy, funds, a timetable, and a way to measure progress.

Here are the nine steps:

1. What is it we want to accomplish? (goals)
2. How will we know when we've arrived? (metrics)
3. Knowing the target audience (potential donors)
4. Share your passion (message)
5. Who's going to do what? (people)
6. What tactics will be employed? (strategy)
7. What will the strategy cost? (funds)
8. When do the activities take place? (timetable)
9. Are we there yet? (measure progress)

- ***What is it we want to accomplish?*** Goals can be audacious: but they need to be reasonable, attainable, and measurable. God can do what He desires through us, with us, or in spite of our efforts. Too far-reaching or fuzzy goals will be challenging to defend if things go wrong. Set goals that are in line with past performance. If this is your first rodeo, sprinkle in some reality and caution. It's essential to reach the set goals or at least to come as close as possible. (**Chapter 16—Goal Setting: Dream Big!** details goal setting.)

- ***How will we know when we've arrived?*** It's essential to distinguish vanity numbers and actionable metrics. When people "Like" our Facebook or Instagram posts, we cheer. When the visitor traffic to our website climbs, we get excited. Both occurrences are noteworthy. But are the numbers actionable? Are they moving us closer to our goal? (**Chapter 17: Metrics—Traffic, Conversions, Average Gifts—Oh My**, talks about choosing numbers that tell the true story of progress.)

- ***Knowing the target audience.*** Knowing how the audience reacts to the fundraising effort and their passions and expectations is paramount. Missing what's important to the donors may cause the fundraising plan to fail miserably. Hopefully, communication and engagement will occur all year before implementing the year-end plan.

(**Chapter 14: Development—Making New Friends** deals with knowing your target audience.)

- **Share your passion.** One must tell a great story to get people's attention in this noisy world. Great stories have a "purpose." Draw the reader into what's said. The story shares intimate details the reader is interested in hearing. The storyline invokes interest, passion, and emotion. Don't bore the reader by rambling, wandering, or droning on and on. The reader should not doubt what action you want them to take by the story's end. (**Chapter 17: Storytelling—Sharing Your Passion** examines what it takes to tell a great story.)

- **Who's going to do what?** An introverted person may not be the best choice to run the social media effort, nor is a person without good communication skills the safest option for writing marketing pieces. If needed, take stock of the team's skills and bring others on board. (**Chapter 6: Personnel—Readying the Team**, talked about having the right people in the correct positions.)

- **What tactics will be employed?** Match the tactics used to communicate the message to the team's skills. Don't push the group into social media and aggressive email marketing campaigns if the group is low-tech. Letters, phone calls (or Zoom calls), and meetings over coffee and tea might work best. Choose more than one way to communicate with people. Some people will pay attention to letters mailed versus reading what drops in their inboxes. (**Chapter 18: Strategy—Planning Your Ground Game** helps you through the planning process.)

- *What will the strategy cost?* Develop a fundraising budget. Think about having a significant donor underwrite the cost of some of the fundraising expenses. (**Chapter 8—Budgeting: Counting the Cost** focused on creating a budget.)

- *When do the activities take place?* Putting the timeline together first and then picking the starting date is always better. It doesn't make sense to wait until October to build the year-end fundraising plan, which takes five months to execute. Be sensitive and do not overload any one team member. Make sure everyone involved understands the assignments, milestones, and due dates. Be flexible. If parts of the plan need more time, make every attempt to move things around, keeping the end goals in mind. (**Chapter 18: Strategy—Planning Your Ground Game** highlights plan execution.)

- *Measuring your progress* – Knowing you're heading in the right direction and making good progress is essential. Decide on the factors that mean the most to the success of the fundraising effort and track those numbers closely. Be willing to turn off marketing efforts that are not producing positive results and keep the best tactics. (**Chapter 19: Analysis—Are We There Yet?** looks at how we can tell if we've achieved our goals)

If you can't see fundraising as more than asking people for money, you may want to check out Guy Burgo's book, *Free to Give as God Intended: A Biblical Look at Christian Giving.*

Ministries X, Y, and Z

In the following six chapters, we'll take three made-up ministries through the prescribed nine-step process to see how what we've learned works together.

Because we've already covered three of those nine elements in past chapters, we'll include insights from **Chapter 6: Personnel—Readying the Team**, **Chapter 8: Budgeting—Counting the Cost**, and **Chapter 14: Development—Making New Friends**. In this way, the process we take the three made-up organizations through will hang together.

Ministry X desires to boost donor acquisition. Suppose Ministry X wants to add 1,000 new donors to their file.

Ministry Y is planning to launch an end-of-the-year fundraising campaign. Ministry Y has big plans for the coming year to raise $200,000 by December 31st.

Ministry Z has decided to publish a three-book series called *The Ministry Roadmap Series*. The first book will be titled **Starting A Ministry,** followed by **Running A Ministry** and **Growing A Ministry**.

Read along as we take the ministries through the nine steps.

— 16 —

Goal Setting:
Dream Big!

What You'll Learn:

- **Learn** why the psychology of goal setting makes sense.
- **Learn** why writing goals down can determine the project's outcome.
- **Learn** how to tell if the goals are achievable.

Goals are critical. They motivate us. They set our direction. They give us focus. They inspire us to do more than we believe we can. Reaching goals helps solve problems. They give us a way to measure our progress. Goals also help to eliminate procrastination.

If we think about goal setting, we can break the process down into these elements:

- Set goals that motivate.
- Use the S.M.A.R.T. method when setting your goals.
- Write the goals down.
- Develop an action plan to achieve the goals.
- Stay focused—don't get sidetracked.

 Goals need to be in line with an organization's mission.

Set Goals That Motivate

An organization's goals must inspire the team and stir their passion. The goals must excite the team and create a sense of urgency to complete the mission.

The team members must understand what achieving the goals means to the recipients. The organization feeds orphans, shares the Good News, trains pastors, digs water wells, and starts micro businesses. We raise people's quality of life. More people enter God's Kingdom.

 The team members need to know the reasons behind the goals.

Use the S.M.A.R.T. Method When Setting Your Goals

If you're unfamiliar with the S.M.A.R.T. goal-setting method, it consists of five ingredients. Goals must be specific, measurable, attractive, relevant, and time-bound.

Specific – A non-specific, fuzzy goal generates little or no interest, traction, or gifts. A pregnancy resource center might go with a plea to raise $150,000 by December 31 to save 550 babies in the coming year. Their goal is simple and spelled out. They're raising **$150,000** by **December 31** to **save 550 babies**.

If your project needs to support 50 orphans for the coming year and costs $35 per child per month, the tagline is prominent – **$21,000** by **December 31** cares for **50 Orphans**.

Suppose we say you're building a wall around the girl's dormitory in an unsafe part of town, and the construction cost is $9,000. Put together a campaign to raise **$3,000** monthly for three months. People like deadlines.

Don't only ask people to donate money. People may have the funds to give. At other times, they may be unable to support the effort financially. Give people different ways to invest their time, talent, and treasure. Perhaps they can be a regular volunteer, a one-time helper, or part of the fundraising committee.

Don't use dollar amounts people cannot relate to. Break the amount down so people can grasp the sum of money. Everyone can relate to the cost of their morning latte, a dinner out, or the price of theater tickets.

 Be specific. Provide people with giving options.

If part of the campaign will be to acquire more email addresses of prospective or actual donors, then those numbers should also be specific.

Suppose we consider these numbers:

- Increase the size of your donor file by 20%.
- Acquire the email addresses of 100 new prospective donors.
- Increase the number of donors that do direct deposit by 20%.
- Increase the number of monthly donors by 10.
- Acquire one more anchor donor.

Don't worry if the estimate is off.

If you don't have a long history to look back on, the odds are your estimates, as specific as you might think they are, maybe high or low.

You won't be able to tell if your estimates are misaligned until things are underway and you can gauge the success rate in reaching those guesstimates.

<u>Measurable</u> – Progress needs to be measured. When checking the roadmap, it's easy to tell when you're halfway to the destination. If the year-end goal is to raise **$30,000** over the **60 days** between **November and December**, divide the total sum between the nine weeks that comprise that period. If, after three weeks, the fundraising effort has not raised $10,000, it will be evident to everyone on the team that the fundraising is not on track. Adjust the goal.

Yes, it's great that more people "like" your Facebook page or visit the website, but are they acting? Are they leaving their email addresses behind, donating, or joining the venture?

Measure numbers that contribute to reaching the goals—not vanity numbers. Numbers that may make you feel good but are not producing any results.

<u>Attainable</u> – Goals need to be feasible. If you're setting goals for the first time, you must mix reality and good fortune with a bit of guesswork. Ask around. Ask God. Find out the average fundraising goal for a project of your size. How successful were others that came before you?

You may need to raise $50,000 to get everything done on your list of projects. But that doesn't mean you'll be able to raise the money in one fundraising round.

Let's look at a "for instance."

Suppose your fundraising efforts last year raised $20,000, and the year before, $35,000 was raised. The likelihood of raising $50,000 during the current year's campaigns is most unlikely unless you plan on stepping up your fundraising activities significantly.

Suppose we imagine you have no fundraising history to look back on. How do you estimate your goal? You seek counsel, pray, and then make your best guess.

Using the same analogy, assume you want to raise $50,000 in the coming year. This year, if you raise $15,000 or $20,000 halfway through the year, the possibility of meeting the $50,000 goal may be out of reach unless things change.

Set your goals as exact as possible, monitor their progress closely, and make changes when necessary if you fall short. Either dial the goals back or step up the fundraising activities.

Settings goals that are not achievable only demoralize team members. Similarly, don't set goals where no one needs to work hard and there are few challenges.

 Always leave room for God to work.

Set realistic goals. Again, after expending 25% or 30% of the effort, it will be evident whether the initial goals are attainable. If your fundraising goal is off, adjust and learn from it.

Relevant – It's important to remember that the fundraising goals must align with your organization's overall vision and mission.

If there are disconnects between the work and the organization's vision and mission, donors may find it hard to support the group's efforts financially.

 People have little interest in achieving goals if the objectives are not directly related to what they're passionate about.

It's easy to get off track when setting goals. At times, the work can be overwhelming. What needs accomplishing may be more than the organization can handle.

Stay true to your initial vision and mission. It's better to take on additional projects or expand one's purpose once fundraising is successful.

Make sure every team member buy into the fundraising objectives, or disharmony and a lack of enthusiasm may be around the corner.

___Time Bound___ – Assume we use the end-of-the-year for this example. Without deadlines, few projects are finished on time or at all. The deadline for end-of-the-year fundraising is December 31. Because our end-of-the-year fundraising runs for several months, breaking the fundraising effort into smaller chunks makes sense. For instance, we might start brainstorming ideas about our E.O.Y. fundraising effort in August, do the goal setting in September, plan the marketing tactics in October, launch the effort in November, and push hard to a conclusion in December.

When planning the year-end effort, remember what is already happening in the organization. Don't overload team members.

 Solicit input from others to make sure the deadlines are realistic and achievable.

 Make allowances for the unforeseen. The unexpected will always rear its ugly head at the most inopportune times.

Write Down the Goals

A plan worth doing merits recording. The written plan can be simple or exhaustive—you decide. A simple fundraising plan might include the tasks, the resources needed, and who will do what and when. It may not need to be more complex than that.

You might use an online project management app to track the deadlines or a WORD document or EXCEL spreadsheet to track things.

Don't tie yourself to a system that manages you instead of you being in charge. More than a few project management systems demand loads of time before they spit out the needed information.

Stay Focused—
Don't Get Sidetracked

Goal setting is an ongoing process. As the fundraising process proceeds, things may need adjustment. The original estimates may be too high or too low.

Perhaps the email campaigns are working better than the Facebook ads. If that's the case, turn off what's not working and boost what is showing positive results.

Resist what's known in the industry as scope creep. That's

where people take their eye off the ball and start going in different directions or expand the original goals too far.

Try to handle one pressing issue at a time, do it well—Everything with Excellence, then move on.

Constantly recast the vision and keep the group excited about reaching the goals.

How to Tell If the Goals Are Achievable

Numbers tell the real story. They separate reality from feelings. Whether trying to enlist 50 volunteers for the Summer 5K Run, 100 new donors for the coming year, or raising $52,000 for the year's building projects, numbers tell the story of success or failure.

Team members won't know where they're heading if the goals are vague. Supporters will be unsure of the organization's objectives.

If the intents are indefinite and not **measurable**, everyone may have a different idea of how well things are going.

If the aims are not **attainable**, team members will become disillusioned. Donors may withdraw their support.

Potential donors and regular supporters may bail from the effort if intentions are incompatible and irrelevant. Team members may wonder why the actions are even taking place.

 If deadlines are non-existent instead of time-bound, people may wonder if they'll ever arrive at the finish line.

Let's set goals for our three made-up ministries.

Ministry X Goal Setting Example (1)

Ministry X Goal Setting Example
"Everything with Excellence"

Project One: Ministry X desires to boost donor acquisition by 1,000 new supporters within a 90-day period. Their unsure of which tactics will produce the best results. They plan on developing several pilot projects and then measure the outcomes. The proposed avenues include: 1.) Facebook Ads, 2.) Peer-to-peer name acquisition with existing donors. 3.) Expanding the organizations reach through social media, 4.) Ask board members for assistance on who they may know, 5.) Make the website content a priority, and 6.) Write guest posts on influencer sites. (These items are in no order of priority or importance.)

Individual landing pages will need to be designed so the locations where the donors are coming from can be identified.

To make sure the ministry understands the today's donor community, they plan on developing a survey to administer to their current donors to what they can learn before launching their acquisition pilot projects.

Specific:

- A 10-question survey will be developed to gain donor knowledge.
- An information packet will be developed and at the next meeting, board members will be taken through the information and asked to meet with their friends and associates.
- The same information packet will be made available to current donors who are willing to set up peer-to-peer appointments.
- Facebooks ads will be investigated along with ways to expand the ministries reach on its current social channels.
- The website content will be updated, and the search engine optimization (SEO) will be checked.
- A series of articles will be written. Influencer sites will be researched. And emails will be sent out looking for guest-post opportunities.

Measurable:

- Hopefully all board members will agree solicit involvement from their friends and colleagues. There are currently 8 board members. If each one asks 10 of their contacts and half show interest in the ministry 40 new donors could be added to the database.
- Currently 3,200 people donate to the ministry. If 20% show interest in doing peer-to-peer fundraising, 640 new donors could be added.
- Facebook ad campaigns will run for 4 weeks. The acquisition target is 250 new donors. 100 new supporters is the target from regular Facebook and Instagram posts.
- 50 new donors are estimated after the website is updated, and the SEO is applied.
- 50 new supporters is the estimate from doing guest posts.

Copyright © 2019 ministryTHRIVE

Ministry X Goal Setting Example (2)

Attainable:
- Board members have not been previously asked to do peer-to-peer fundraising, so the target may not be realistic.
- In the past, current donors have been successful in helping to acquire between 500 and 825 new donors. The 640 number is seen to be attainable.
- The ministry has not sought new donors from Facebook ads and or the social platforms. The estimate of 350 new donors may not be met.
- Website SEO has always produced new donors.
- Writing guest posts has always been successful in the past.

Relevant:
- Content, stories, and posts will be developed in line with donor passions.
- Insight gleaned from the survey will be added to the content.

Time Bound:
- Develop donor survey by March 1. Administer survey by March 7. Review survey results and develop new content, stories, and posts. March 15 through April 15.
- Develop information package by April 30. Give to board members and current donors.
- Create Facebook ads and social content between April 30 and May 30.
- SEO website by April 1.
- Write guest posts and look for influencer partners by May 1.

Copyright © 2019 ministryTHRIVE

Ministry Y Goal Setting Example

Ministry Y Goal Setting Example
"Everything with Excellence"

Project One: Launch an End-of-the-year Fundraising Campaign. Suppose the ministry's goal is to support 50 new orphans for the coming year. Today it costs $35 per child per month. The tagline the ministry developed is: **$21,000** by **December 31**st cares for **50 Orphans**. They plan on raising the funds through their current donor base. Ministry Y currently has 500 donors. They plan on using three tactics: a mailer, email campaign and phone calls.

Specific:

- The tagline, **$21,000** by **December 31**st cares for **50 Orphans** will be prominent on the website and social pages.
- Mailers will be designed around the tagline.
- An email campaign will be developed and launched during November and December.
- Phone calls will be placed to regular monthly and major donors.

Measurable:

- In the past, 25% of the donation have come in from the mailer and the email campaign.
- 75% of the donations have come from personal phone calls and one-on-one meetings.

Attainable:

- In the past two years, Ministry Y has been able to raise $18,000 and $34,000. 21,000 is definitely within reach.

Relevant:

- Ministry Y stays in close contact with its donors through its monthly newsletter and social channels. They have a good handle on donor passions.

Time Bound:

- Mailer will be designed by November 1 and sent out by November 15.
- The email campaign will be run between November 30 and December 15.
- Personal calls and meetings will take place during the month of December.

Copyright © 2019 ministryTHRIVE

Ministry Z Goal Setting Example

Ministry Z Goal Setting Example
"Everything with Excellence"

Project One:
Launch the Ministry Blueprint Series. Starting A Ministry, targets ministries that have been in existence for 6 to 18 months. Running A Ministry and Growing a Ministry are for ministries that are struggling with either operations or grow. Three avenues will be used to promote the book: a workshop, Amazon, and a webinar.

Specific:

- The first book in this series will focus on what it takes to start or build a thriving, sustainable ministry.
- Develop and hold workshops based on the learnings.
- Collect feedback to ensure the materials are most useful.
- Develop a slide deck and present a Go-to-Meeting webinar to introduce the educational materials to projects worldwide. It is important the webinar be available on-demand.
- Use KDP (Amazon.com) to publish and sell the books. Include examples, worksheets, info card and other documents to give projects a jumpstart on creating their own fundraising materials.

Measurable:

- The workshop – 80 attendees on April 15, 2019
- The book – sell 300 copies by June 30, 2019, sell 1,000 copies by September 31, 2019
- The webinar – 400 downloads by September 1, 2019, 1K downloads by December 31, 2019

Attainable:

- 200 projects have been identified in the state of Colorado. Hopefully 80 will attend the April 15, 2019 webinar.

Relevant:

- Book chapters: What's Your Why?, Turning Your Passion into Purpose, Doing Your Homework, Getting Legit—Staying Legit, Readying the Team, Gotcha Covered, Counting the Cost………… , Looking Good, Sharing Your Passion, Being Seen in All the Right Places, Talking the Talk, Walking the Walk, Making New Friends, Ministry Takes Money, Dream Big!, Are We There Yet?, Sharing Your Passion, Planning Your Ground Game , Executing Your Plan, Measuring Your Progress, "I've Got Your Back", The Balancing Act, Before I Go

Time Bound:

- Finish book manuscript by March 1, 2019
- Finish webinar slide deck by March 10, 2019
- Ready book for publishing and sale by April 1, 2019
- Hold webinar on April 15, 2019
- Announce book for sale on April 15, 2019.

Copyright © 2019 ministryTHRIVE

S.M.A.R.T. Goal Setting Worksheet

S.M.A.R.T. Goal Setting Worksheet

"Everything with Excellence"

Project One: _____

Specific: _____
_____
_____

Measurable: _____
_____
_____

Attainable: _____
_____
_____

Relevant: _____
_____
_____

Time Bound: _____
_____
_____

Copyright © 2019 ministryTHRIVE

Setting Practical Priorities

Setting S.M.A.R.T. goals is vital. Prioritizing those objectives is also necessary. No team can work on all the projects at once.

Every ministry lacks resources, funds, talent, or time during a typical year. Priorities must be set so the most essential items (goals) get attention first.

 Can more than one project be worked on at the same time? Of course. It takes planning, resource allocation, and scheduling.

Answer these questions:

1. Which project moves us closer to our overall vision?
2. Which project are we best suited for?
3. Which project will have the most impact?
4. Which project is the best use of our resources? (time, talent, treasure)

Think about using this simple priority-setting scale:

Priority 1: Must do. These goals define your success.
Priority 2: Should do. These goals are not essential but would be great to accomplish.

Priority 3: Nice to do. Self-explanatory.

Suppose we develop priority worksheets for Ministries X, Y, and Z.

Ministry X Project Priority Example

Ministry X Project Priority Example

"Everything with Excellence"

Project One: Develop donor survey by March 1. Administer survey by March 7. Review survey results and develop new content, stories, and posts. March 15 through April 15.

Urgency: Multiple dates   Cost: $0   Priority: 1

Project Two: SEO website by April 1.

Urgency: April 1, 2019   Cost: $0   Priority: 2

Project Three: Develop information package by April 30. Give to board members and current donors.

Urgency: April 30, 2019   Cost: $0   Priority: 3

Project Four: Create Facebook ads and social content between April 30 and May 30.

Urgency: Multiple dates   Cost: $500   Priority: 4

Project Five: Write guest posts and look for influencer partners by May 1.

Urgency: May 1, 2019   Cost: $0   Priority: 5

Copyright © 2019 ministryTHRIVE

Ministry Y Project Priority Example

Ministry Y Project Priority Example

"Everything with Excellence"

Project One: Mailer will be designed by November 1 and sent out by November 15.

Urgency: Mixed dates   Cost: $150   Priority: 1

Project Two: The email campaign will be will run between November 30 and December 15.

Urgency: Mixed dates   Cost: $0   Priority: 2

Project Three: Personal calls and meeting will take place during the month of December.

Urgency: Mixed dates   Cost: $0   Priority: 3

Copyright © 2019 ministryTHRIVE

Starting A Ministry

Ministry Z Project Priority Example

Ministry Z Project Priority Example

"Everything with Excellence"

Project One: Finish book manuscript.

Urgency: March 1, 2019   Cost: $0   Priority: 1

Project Two: Finish webinar slide deck.

Urgency: March 10, 2019   Cost: $0   Priority: 2

Project Three: Ready book for publishing and sale.

Urgency: April 1, 2019   Cost: $0   Priority: 3

Project Four: Hold webinar.

Urgency: April 15, 2019   Cost: $0   Priority: 4

Project Five: Announce book for sale.

Urgency: April 15, 2019   Cost: $0   Priority: 5

Copyright © 2019 ministryTHRIVE

Project Priority Worksheet

Project Priority Worksheet

"Everything with Excellence"

Project One: _____
_____

Urgency: _____   Cost: _____   Priority: _____

Project Two: _____
_____

Urgency: _____   Cost: _____   Priority: _____

Project Three: _____
_____

Urgency: _____   Cost: _____   Priority: _____

Project Four: _____
_____

Urgency: _____   Cost: _____   Priority: _____

Project Five: _____
_____

Urgency: _____   Cost: _____   Priority: _____

Copyright © 2019 ministryTHRIVE

– 17 –

Storytelling: Sharing Your Passion

What You'll Learn:

- **Learn** how you can become a great storyteller.
- **Learn** how the nine storytelling elements play a role in holding the reader's attention and bringing them to a decision to give or take no action.
- **Learn** why there is no substitute for including a few snapshots and impactful stories from those being affected by the ministry's efforts.

There's no substitute for telling a compelling story that gets positive results. Everyone loves hearing or reading a great story.

An organization can spend its entire fundraising budget on Facebook ads or weekly email salvos. But without a great story attached, the fundraising outcome will likely be disappointing.

Telling a great story draws the reader in. It leaves no doubt in the reader's mind about how the donated money is making an enormous impact.

  Write, then edit. It's nearly impossible to constantly stop the creative process and shift gears to the diagnostic phase (editing).

Here's a list of thoughts that come to mind when thinking about constructing a great story:

- Every great story has a purpose.
- Every great story has a hook.
- Every great story draws the reader into the story as soon as possible.
- Don't wander.
- Keep it real by using "hero" photos and exact details.
- Brief storytelling works best.
- Tap into the reader's emotions.
- Does the reader see their self in this situation?
- Brings in those being affected.

Let's examine the elements that make up a great story:

Every Great Story Has a Purpose

Whether in an email, newsletter, Facebook ad, or blog post, the question is, "Why are you writing this story in the first place?" There needs to be a goal, a reason, an intent. Why are you wasting your time and energy asking the reader to invest theirs? The goal might be to educate potential donors. It may be to encourage people to get involved in the work at a deeper level. You might be making a plea at the end of the year.

 Decide on the goals before the writing begins.

Have a Hook

Every great story has a hook, usually the book's first sentence. The "hook" grabs the reader's attention and piques their curiosity. They end up wanting to know more. Harper Lee starts *To Kill a Mockingbird* by writing, "When he was nearly thirteen, my brother Jem got his arm badly broken at the elbow." Wow, what happened? J. R. R. Tolkien starts The Hobbit this way, "In a hole in the ground there lived a hobbit. Not a dirty, nasty, wet hole, filled with the ends of worms and an oozy smell, nor yet a dry, bare, sandy hole with nothing to sit down on or eat it was a hobbit hole, and that means comfort."

Craft a compelling first sentence (or headline), and you're well on your way to grabbing the reader's attention and telling a great story.

Draw the Reader into the Story as Soon as Possible

Draw the reader into the story without using words like ours and us. Those words tend to remove the reader from the story. Use language the reader is familiar with seeing. Don't get bogged down in too many details too soon. Start to develop a storyline. Let the reader know where you're taking them. The reader is investing time. They need to know you won't be wasting it.

 Surveys state the average human attention span is approximately 8 seconds.

Don't Wander

Avoid introducing too many facets of what's happening on the ground, even though they all may be exciting. The reader may become confused. If you have several accounts, write several short, separate stories. Stay at a level of detail familiar to the reader and avoid getting too far into the weeds.

 Get over your perfectionist tendencies. Just write.

Keep It Real by Using Photos and Exact Details

Photos of the location or action shots create interest. Posed pictures of children standing outside their orphanage do little to bring excitement to a story. Children playing, standing in line to receive their shots, or receiving gift packages end up showcasing the project's impact. Few things warm a person's heart more than seeing children smiling, playing, or having fun. These are known as "hero" photos.

 Tell people what's happening in the photos; don't assume.

Brief Storytelling Works Best

There's no reason to compile a novelette when a short story will do. People's time is precious, and competition for their attention is fierce.

There are accepted writing standards out there; follow them. A newsletter can be longer than a blog post. A post on Facebook can be longer than the text associated with a picture sent on Instagram. Stick with what everyone is expecting. Emails that droll on are hardly ever finished or started, for that matter. Long emails are usually placed in the recipient's trash folder before being read.

Tap into the Reader's Emotions

It's important to share your passion for what God is doing and tap into the reader's emotions. Don't keep things dry and detached. How is the work affecting the lives of the people on the ground? Talk about the victories as well as the challenges. Talk about changing lives. Share your feelings and the feelings of the beneficiaries.

Can the Reader See Their Self in this Situation?

Try and find ways for the reader to see themselves in the story. Can they see themselves doing the work? Can they see themselves as happy as you are when describing the events? Remember, there may be a great distance between the reader and what's happening overseas. That gap needs to be closed as much as possible.

Bring in Those Being Affected

There is no natural substitute for hearing from the families or children touched positively by the organization's efforts. A quote or two within the story lends incredible veracity to the tale. Take action photos to show what's taking place on the ground.

Use "hero" photos whenever possible.

Telling a Great Story Worksheet (1)

Telling a Great Story
Worksheet

Okay, now that we have a good idea of what goes into telling a great story, let's answer the seven questions that opened this chapter. First, jot down your ideas on these Show & Tell pages. Then open a document and start writing.

Here's a writing tip: Don't write and edit at the same time. First let the ideas flow, and then come back and put your editor's hat on to polish the copy.

What's our purpose in writing?

_____
_____
_____

How do we make the story compelling?

_____
_____
_____

How can we share our passion?

_____
_____
_____

How do we keep it real with photos and stories?

_____
_____
_____

Copyright © 2019 ministryTHRIVE

Telling a Great Story
Worksheet (2)

How do we tap into the donor's (reader's) emotions?

_____
_____
_____

How can the donor see themselves in the story?

_____
_____
_____

Copyright © 2019 ministryTHRIVE

– 18 –

Strategy: Planning Your Ground Game

What You'll Learn:

- **Learn** the subtle difference between strategies, goals, and objectives.
- **Learn** why executing with excellence determines the mission's success.
- **Learn** the importance of matching the tasks at hand with people's skills.

A quick recap before we get into **Planning Your Ground Game**. In **Chapter 16: Goal Setting—Dream Big,** we discussed the importance of setting goals and priorities.

Chapters 6 and 8 cover budgets and personnel, both vital elements of planning one's ground game.

Plans can be simple or complex. They can have a half-dozen steps or be more complicated. You make the decision.

 Go with a plan format that suits your organization best.

Organizations that are more mature and better staffed may achieve their goals by using their website, social media channels, and email campaigns.

Suppose we focus on using email campaigns to achieve our stated goals.

Plans typically comprise goals, objectives, skills, responsibilities, schedules (timing and deadlines), resources, and a budget.

Let's take a moment to define some terms so we're all on the same page. The **goal** is the outcome we hope to achieve. The **strategy** is the plan or approach employed to achieve the goal. An **objective** is a measurable step one takes to move toward accomplishing the overall strategy.

Suppose we aim to add 1,000 new email addresses to our contact file over the next 60 days.

With that in mind, we might run four email campaigns over a 60-day timeframe. Each campaign could be considered an *objective*.

 The organization must try to match the responsibilities to the people with the necessary skills.

Now that we've settled on the goals and objectives, it's on to skills, responsibilities, schedules, resources, and budget.

The organization must try to match the **responsibilities** to people with the necessary **skills**. Don't ask the person with little or no technical know-how to handle the duties of running the email automation platform.

In the same vein, if a person dislikes writing, they will not be the best candidate to draft the email messages.

Schedules and meeting **deadlines** must be reached on time. Sending emails with no timetable only confuses the recipients and will not produce the desired results.

Timing matters. Suppose we say the best time to send the emails out is between nine and ten o'clock in the morning on Tuesdays, Wednesdays, or Thursdays. So, sending the messages out late Friday afternoon will surely spell disaster for the campaign.

Here's another sample email plan. It mentions the email number, the timing, and the purpose of each communique.

- Email 1. Sent out upon registering for the free training. This email confirms their sign-up.
- Email 2. Sent out on Day 1. Welcomes the student.
- Email 3. Sent out on Day 3. Focuses on a major feature that benefits the student.
- Email 4. Sent out on Day 7. Focuses on a second major feature.
- Email 5. Sent out on Day 11. Focuses on a third important feature.
- Email 6. Sent out on Day 13. Focuses on a fourth prominent feature.
- Email 7. Sent out on Day 15. Let the student know the free trial is expiring.
- Email 8. Sent out on Day 17. Makes the student aware of a special offer if they enroll.

Finally, there's the issue of **budget**. Luckily, many email automation platforms have free trials or free-forever memberships. For instance, at the writing of this book, MailChimp.com offers the best free-forever option if the organization does not email more than 2,000 contacts. iContact.com has a 30-day free trial, while ConstantContact.com provides a free 60-day experience.

Ministry X Action Plan Schedule Example

	A	B	C	D	E	F
1		Ministry X Action Plan Schedule Example				
2	2019	Task	Person	Deadline	Actual	Comments
3		**Develop Donor Survey**				
4		Develop survey		1-Mar		
5		Administer survey		7-Mar		
6		Review results		10-Mar		
7		**Information Packet**				
8		Draft packet content		10-Apr		
9		Finalize content packet		15-Apr		
10		Send to board		30-Apr		
11		Board member meetings		30-May		
12		Gather statistics		1-Jun		
13		**Social Content**				
14		Draft content ideas		15-Apr		
15		Ceate content		30-Apr		
16		Post content		30-May		
17		Track social channels		1-Jun		
18		**Facebook Ads**				
19		Draft ad content		10-Apr		
20		Design ads		20-Apr		
21		Decide on audiences		25-Apr		
22		Upload ads		28-Apr		
23		Turn ads on		30-Apr		
24		Track ads		ongoing		
25		End ad campaigns		30-May		
26		Gather statistics		1-Jun		
27		**Optimize Website**				
28		Draft optimization		1-Mar		
29		Apply optimization		15-Mar		
30		Finalize SEO		1-Apr		
31		**Write Guest Posts**				
32		Identify influencers		5-Mar		
33		Email influencers to gage interest		15-Mar		
34		Develop writing topics		1-Apr		
35		Draft guest posts		15-Apr		
36		Review/edit guest posts		25-Apr		
37		Send guest posts to influencers		1-May		
38		Gather statistics		1-Jun		
39						

Ministry Y Action Plan Schedule Example

	2019	Task	Person	Deadline	Actual	Comments
1		**Mailer**				
2		Draft mailer		5-Oct		
3		Send mailer around for comment		15-Oct		
4		Finalize mailer		1-Nov		
5		Send out mailer		15-Nov		
6		**Email Campaign**				
7		Create subscribe landing page		5-Nov		
8		Finalize landing page		10-Nov		
9		Upload email addresses to MailChimp		15-Nov		
10		Draft emails		20-Nov		
11		Finalize emails		25-Nov		
12		Begin email campaign		30-Nov		
13		Conclude email campaign		15-Dec		
14		Gather statistics		16-Dec		
15		**Personal Calls & Meetings**				
16		Develop list for calls		25-Nov		
17		Develop list for meetings		25-Nov		
18		Start calls & meetings		1-Dec		
19		Conclude calls & meetings		31-Dec		

Ministry Z Action Plan Schedule Example

	A	B	C	D	E	F
1			Ministry Z Action Plan Schedule Example			
2	2019	Task	Person	Deadline	Actual	Comments
3		**Starting A Ministry manuscript**				
4		Draft manuscript		25-Jan		
5		Complete first edit		1-Feb		
6		Complete second edit		8-Feb		
7		Solicit comments		15-Feb		
8		Make final edits		22-Feb		
9		Finish manuscript		1-Mar		
10		**Ready Book for Sale**				
11		Upload manuscript to KDP		15-Mar		
12		Review uploaded copy		22-Mar		
13		Make final edits		29-Mar		
14		Post book for sale		1-Apr		
15		**Create Workshop/Webinar Slides**				
16		Draft slide outline		10-Feb		
17		Draft slides		15-Feb		
18		Finalize slides		20-Feb		
19		Email slides to Board for comment		25-Feb		
20		**Do Workshop Run-through**				
21		Do run-through		1-Mar		
22		Record feedback		5-Mar		
23		Adjust slide content accordingly		10-Mar		
24		**Do Webinar**				
25		Present workshop		15-Apr		
26		Gather statistics		16-Apr		
27		Present Webinar		20-Apr		
28						

Action Plan Schedule Worksheet

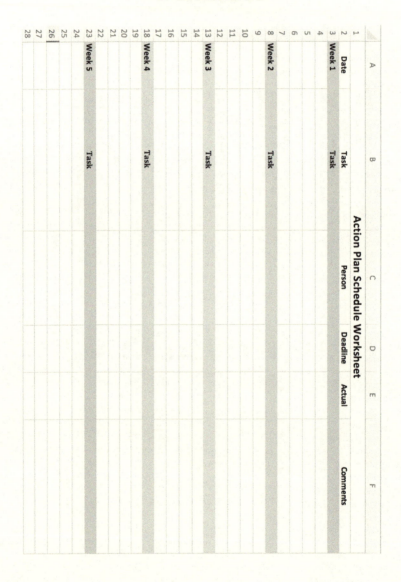

— 19 —

Analysis:
Are We There Yet?

What You'll Learn:

- **Learn** the difference between traffic, conversions, and average gift size.
- **Learn** how to measure the numbers that tell the real story.
- **Learn** how to tell which communication channels (face-to-face meetings, websites, support letters, newsletters, emails, or social media) are producing the best results.

Don't attempt to measure feelings or emotions—measure numbers. What needs to be measured to show real success? Yes, we could look at the amount of funds raised, but that won't tell us where we're having the most success and where we're likely wasting our fundraising resources and time.

175 *Traffic, Conversions, Average Gifts—Oh My!*

If gifts are coming in, who's giving? What message is working best? What marketing channel is showing the best results? It's essential to ensure we're measuring the numbers that tell the actual story of what's happening.

Assume we send out 75 newsletters attached to emails. How will we know if people open emails and read what we wrote? They won't.

Use an email marketing automation system like MailChimp.com to send emails, and track opens and click-throughs. This way, we will know exactly how many emails were read. We won't have any idea if we use a mail client like Outlook or Apple's Mail program.

 MailChimp is a free service if you're emailing to fewer than 2,000 contacts per month.

So, what do we measure?

Suppose we're reaching our donors and potential supporters through various channels: the website, support letters, newsletters, emails, social media, and face-to-face meetings. These avenues are not going to show the same success rates.

Suppose we spend a few moments drawing distinctions

between what we'll call **vanity numbers** and **actionable metrics**. Vanity numbers might be the number of pageviews our website received last month or the number of "Likes" our Facebook page garnered this past week.

At first, we care about these numbers, but they're not the numbers we're after in the long run. We care most about the actions people take. Actions include providing their email address or other personal information, downloading our latest newsletter, or donating.

We first need to generate **traffic** and then **conversions**.

Let's break down the more popular ways we communicate with people and look at the numbers that matter most.

Face-to-face Meetings

Face-to-face meetings tend to be the most successful way to acquire new donors.

But we'll have to do analysis and perform diagnostics on the actions and conversations that take place before we can determine our level of success.

Let's analyze a typical face-to-face meeting scenario.

When we ask people if we could meet, they are apt to respond in one of three ways: they'll say "Yes," "No," or "Now's not a good time."

What to do?

For the people who said "Yes," our action is obvious set up a meeting time.

What to do with those who said "No" and "Now's not a good time?"

We could ask if the people who said "No" would support us in prayer. If they respond positively, we could ask if they would not mind if we sent them a few periodic emails to let them know how they could support the efforts on the ground.

For those who said, "Now's not a good time," they might mean now is not a good time, or they may mean No. We won't know until we ask them a second or third question. The second question might be, "Would a time next week work better for you?" If they say "Yes," we can book a time. Suppose they say next week is not good. Then perhaps they're trying to let us down easily but are reluctant to say No. In that case, we revert to asking them to support us in prayer.

The same type of analysis and diagnostic exercises need to

occur during the actual face-to-face meeting and afterward.

We'll want to develop meaningful metrics to determine if our face-to-face meetings are profitable.

If we look at the many ways to communicate and engage people, we could track dozens of metrics. Suppose we keep things simple. Here are the face-to-face meeting metrics that are most important:

- How many appointment calls were made?
- How many people said, "Yes," "No," and "Now's not a good time?"
- How many "Yeses" turned into actual meetings?
- How many "Nos" are being followed up?
- How many "Now's not a good time" turned into later meetings?
- How many new donors were acquired?
- What is the average gift?

With these numbers, we'll be able to tell if meeting potential donors is worth our investment of time.

Knowing how many appointments we book each week or month is essential. It's more telling how many of those people turn into donors. If we set 10 appointments per month and two of those people become donors, then it's easy to calculate that if we want the appointments to generate five new donors each month, then we need to set 25 appointments per month.

So, the number of appointments (**traffic** *per se*) becomes of secondary importance, while the number of people that say "Yes" (**conversions**) is our primary goal. We're also interested in what people give. If the five new donors gifted $500 together, the **average gift** is $100.

Suppose 25 appointments per month is an unrealistic number. In that case, it becomes apparent we need to look to other avenues to help generate the number of new donors we need to acquire during our fundraising campaign.

This same type of analysis and diagnostics needs to take place with each form of communication we use.

 Don't add people to your email list without asking their permission.

Websites

Understand that not only humans visit websites; bots, or computer programs, make up 49.6% of all Internet traffic. There are good bots and not-so-good bots. Google bots are good bots. Google sends bots to all websites to check for recent updates.

Charlatans from countries outside (and inside) the US send bad bots to websites to scrape email addresses to send back SPAM.

Assuming 100 visitors came to your website last week. There is a good chance that almost half of those visitors were not human.

The first order of business for a website owner is to create **traffic** opportunities. Once the right traffic flows to the site, the next step is to encourage that traffic to take a specific action (**conversion**), say watching a video, subscribing to a newsletter, or giving (**average gift**).

Don't believe the phrase, "If you build it, they will come." They won't. There is so much noise on the Internet that the small fish in this gigantic ocean cannot attract the right audience without budgeting a significant amount of money.

Here's an example:

Say you are supporting an orphanage on the African continent. There are 12,900,000 pages when searching for—orphans in Africa. Let's narrow our search to Ghana by surrounding our phrase "supporting orphans Ghana" with quotes. Now, you'll find 647,000 pages. Your browser must list your website in the first three to five positions. If there is any hope, the person searching finds your website.

 Traffic to a website is good. Conversions from that traffic are best.

So, how should the website initially be used to convert potential donors?

Smaller organizations employ websites to add legitimacy to the project and extend the conversation after the first meeting. Say you have an appointment and tell the person you met with to check out the website where they can find out more about what's happening. The website extends the conversation.

Brochures can only tell so much of the story. Blogs, on the other hand, can be updated moment by moment and are a great storytelling tool to drive potential donors to the website.

 Of course, nothing will replace face-to-face meetings as the most effective way to close.

Support Letters

If support letters are sent by US Mail, there is no way to tell if the right people are opening or reading the letters. The only indication of the letter's success is if an addressee responds, perhaps with an email or a gift.

If you prefer to send out support letters by mail, send an email announcing the letter is on its way and follow up with a second email to ensure the person received your communique.

When they reply, you can track the letter's arrival (**traffic**), if they give (**conversion**), and the size of their gift (**average gift**).

If an organization sends 100 support letters and receives three donations, the conversion rate for sending out the support letters is 3%. If the amount given by the three people is $150, then the average gift size is $50.

Remember, a reasonable response rate from support letters is less than 5%.

If constituents hear from you regularly and the newsletters are relevant, the open rate will increase. Regular does not mean once a year. Think more like monthly or bimonthly.

Newsletters

It's best to send newsletters using an email marketing system such as MailChimp for the same reasons we covered earlier. If you're using US Mail, there's no way to tell what's happening at the other end. A MailChimp-like program would be the only way to track the opens to see if people are opening the email that contains your news.

The only way to know if your newsletter efforts are paying off **(conversions)** is to ask the reader to act by visiting your website, "like" your Facebook page, or donate **(average gift)**.

Newsletters are notorious thieves of time and resources. It's important to know if the newsletter is positively affecting your prospective donor. Is what you're writing about provoking them to take some action?

If not, stop publishing. Try another engagement activity.

Emails

CauseVox has published interesting stats on non-profits sending out emails.

- Recipients consider **12%** of emails spam because they do

not have the sender's email address in their address book.
- Recipients open **25.96%** of non-profit emails. The industry rate is only 6%.
- Having social media icons within the email increases click-through rates by as much as **158%**.
- Personalization increases the click-through rate by **14%**.
- Mobile devices open **53%** of the emails.
- Sending out **four** emails monthly instead of **one** increases the click-through rates.

Here are a few more statistics from ConstantContact, another email marketing automation company much like MailChimp:

- Non-profits average a 20% rate of email openings, with a click-through rate of 8%. The average conversion rate of that 8% is between 1.5 and 3.5%.

Let us run a few test numbers using these percentages.

Say we send out 1,000 emails. That means that, on average, 200 people (20%) will open the email. If only 8% of the 200 people click through to the donation page, our number drops to 16. Let's be generous and say 5% of the people do donate; that's less than one person out of 1,000 potential donors.

Don't be discouraged.

Open, click-through, and conversion rates can improve exponentially by consistently sending emails out regularly. Hence, people expect to hear from you and make sure the content is relevant to the reader, impactful, shows progress and has calls to action that are clear and concise.

If we improved the open rate to 50% and the click-through and conversion rates by 20% and 15%, the donation picture would change dramatically. Out of the 1,000 emails, now 500 people open what we've sent. One hundred people would click through, and 15 would donate.

These rates will continue improving as we sharpen our message and approach. Don't lose heart.

Social Media

Let's look at Facebook, for instance. The number of friends and followers we have and the number of "Likes" our stories receive tell us about our **traffic**. These numbers signal a conversion of sorts but not the number we're most interested in seeing. We're more interested in people visiting our website from the Facebook page (**conversion**) to understand better what we're trying to accomplish and donate (**average gift**) once at our site. These are the significant conversion numbers.

If our Facebook page receives 50 new "Likes" per month and five people click through to our website and donate, we could say our conversion rate from Facebook "Likes" is 10%.

Please don't think we're saying numbers are all that is important. But we can't tell we're getting closer to our destination unless we notice the miles traveled. Numbers refer to the amount of progress made. Numbers tell the real story.

The Measuring Your Success spreadsheet (included) helps track where the gifts are coming from. We could also add email addresses to this table and track those.

It's important to know where we're making the most progress so we can divert more resources toward that effort. If things are not working, be willing to change. Hoping things improve hardly ever show better results.

You may be surprised at which communication method shows the best results—be flexible and stay open-minded. Be ready to act on the information. Don't make too many adjustments at one time so you'll be able to tell which adjustment is making the most difference.

Look at Traffic, Conversions, and Average Gift Size Examples for Ministries X, Y, and Z, and then check out Measuring Progress Examples for the three ministries.

Ministry X
Traffic, Conversions, Average Gift Sizes Example

Ministry X
Traffic, Conversions, Average Gift Sizes
Example

Project: Ministry X desires to boost donor acquisition by 1,000 new supporters within a 90-day period. 1.) Facebook Ads, 2.) Peer-to-peer name acquisition with existing donors. 3.) Expanding the organizations reach through social media, 4.) Ask board members for assistance on who they may know, 5.) Make the website content a priority, and 6.) Write guest posts on influencer sites.

Traffic:

1.) *Traffic* could be viewed as the number of people who view the ad or the number of people who click on the ad. The "nameless" number of people who view the ad is really a number that's not actionable.
2.) *Traffic* would be the number of people existing donors share the information packet with.
3.) *Traffic* would be the number of people that visit the social pages.
4.) *Traffic* would be the number of people board members meet with.
5.) *Traffic* would be the number (organic) of people who visit the website because of the improvements made with the search engine optimization.
6.) *Traffic* would be the number of people who viewed the posts. Hopefully, the influencers will be willing to supply you with those numbers.

Conversions:

1.) *Conversions* would be seen as the number of people who clicked on the ads. A second *conversion* number would be those people that took the action that was advertised: joined, subscribed, or donated.
2.) *Conversions* would be the number of donors that took some action: joined, subscribed, or gave.
3.) *Conversions* could be shares, likes, or follows. Or *conversions* could be: joined, subscribed, or gave.
4.) *Conversions* would be the number of donors that took some action: joined, subscribed, or gave.
5.) *Conversions* would be the number of donors that took some action: joined, subscribed, or gave.
6.) *Conversions* would be the number of donors that took some action: joined, subscribed, or gave.

Average Gifts:

Average Gift Size can be looked at two different ways: either individual donors gave more, or a people increased their donations.

Copyright © 2019 ministryTHRIVE

Ministry Y
Traffic, Conversions, Average Gift Sizes Example

Ministry Y
Traffic, Conversions, Average Gift Sizes
Example

Project: Launch an End-of-the-year Fundraising Campaign. Suppose the ministry's goal is to support 50 new orphans for the coming year. Today it costs $35 per child per month. The tagline the ministry developed is: **$21,000** by **December 31st** cares for **50 Orphans**. They plan on raising the funds through their current donor base. Ministry Y currently has 500 donors. They plan on using three tactics: a mailer, email campaign and phone calls.

Traffic:

1.) *Traffic* would be the number of people receiving the mailer.
2.) *Traffic* would be the number of email recipients overall.
3.) *Traffic* would be the number of phone calls that were actually answered. Not the number of voice mails left.

Conversions:

1.) *Conversions* would be the number of people who took some action: joined, subscribed, donated. Because this is a fundraising campaign, the number of people that donated is the significant *conversion* number.
2.) *Conversions* would be the number of people who took some action: joined, subscribed, donated. Yes, it's good that people opened the email along with those that clicked through to the landing page. But those *conversions* did not result in donations.
3.) *Conversions* would be the number of people that took some action: joined, subscribed, or donated.

Average Gifts:

Average Gift Size can be looked at two different ways: either individual donors gave more, or a people increased their donations.

Copyright © 2019 ministryTHRIVE

Ministry Z
Traffic, Conversions, Average Gift Sizes Example

Ministry Z
Traffic, Conversions, Average Gift Sizes
Example

Project: Launch the Ministry Blueprint Series. Starting A Ministry, targets ministries that have been in existence for 6 to 18 months. Running A Ministry and Growing a Ministry are for ministries that are struggling with either operations or grow. Three avenues will be used to promote the book: a workshop, Amazon, and a webinar.

Traffic:

1.) *Traffic* would be the number of people who received the workshop invite.
2.) Not applicable.
3.) *Traffic* would be the number of people who received the webinar invite.

Conversions:

1.) *Conversions* would be the number of people who registered for the workshop.
2.) *Conversions* would be the number of people who purchased the book.
3.) *Conversions* would be the number of people who registered for the webinar.

Average Gifts:

Not applicable.

Copyright © 2019 ministryTHRIVE

Traffic, Conversions, Average Gift Sizes Worksheet

Traffic, Conversions, Average Gift Sizes
Worksheet

Project: Describe the project here...

_____
_____
_____

How will you measure the traffic, conversions, and average gift sizes?

Traffic:
_____
_____
_____
_____

Conversions:
_____
_____
_____
_____

Average Gifts:
_____
_____
_____
_____

Copyright © 2019 ministryTHRIVE

Starting A Ministry

Ministry X Measuring Your Progress Example

	A	B	C	D	E	F	G
1	Ministry X Measuring Your Progress Example						
2		January	February	March	April	May	June
3	Facebook Ads						
4	# of Ads						
5	# of Views						
6	# of Click-throughs						
7	# of Bails						
8	# of Acquisitions						
9	Social Media (Facebook)						
10	# Page Engagement						
11	Page Engagement Rate						
12	# Pages to Watch						
13	# Likes						
14	# Fans						
15	# Acquisitions						
16	# Visits to Website						
17	Face-to-face						
18	# Calls for Appointments						
19	# Appointments Set						
20	# Appointments Made						
21	# Acquisitions						
22	Donations						
23	Website						
24	# Visitors						
25	# Pages/Sessions						
26	Average Session Duration						
27	C# lick-throughs						
28	% of New Sessions						
29	# Acquisitions						
30	Donations						
31	Guest Posts						
32	# Influencers						
33	# Guest Posts						
34	# Views						
35	# Likes						
36	# of Shares						
37	# of Tweets						
38	# of Comments						
39	# Acquisitions						
40	Donations						
41							

Ministry Y Measuring Your Progress Example

	A	B	C	D	E	F	G
1	Ministry Y Measuring Your Progress Example							
2		January	February	March	April	May	June
3	Email						
4	# Recipients						
5	# Emails sent						
6	# Emails opened						
7	C# lick-throughs						
8	Donations						
9	# Unsubscribes						
10	Mailer						
11	# Recipients						
12	# Landing Page Visits						
13	# Bails						
14	# Click-throughs						
15	Donations						
16	Face-to-face						
17	# Calls for Appointments						
18	# Appointments Set						
19	# Appointments Made						
20	# New Donors Acquired						
21	Donations						
22							
23							
24							
25							
26							
27							
28							
29							
30							
31							
32							

Ministry Z Measuring Your Progress Example

	A	B	C	D	E	F
1		Ministry Z Measuring Your Progress Example				
2		January				
3	Workshop					
4		# Invites				
5		# Registrations				
6		# Attendees				
7		# Book Sales				
8	Webinar					
9		# Invites				
10		# Registrations				
11		# Attendees				
12		# Book Sales				
13						
14						
15						
16						
17						
18						
19						
20						
21						
22						
23						
24						
25						
26						
27						

Measuring Your Progress Worksheet

	A	B	C	D	E	F	G
1		\multicolumn{6}{l}{Measuring Your Progress Worksheet}					
2		January	February	March	April	May	June
3	Website						
4	Visitors						
5	Pages/Sessions						
6	Average Session Duration						
7	Click-throughs						
8	% of New Sessions						
9	Donations						
10	Support Letter						
11	Recipients						
12	Support Letters sent						
13	Support Letters opened						
14	Click-throughs						
15	Donations						
16	Unsubscribes						
17	Newsletter						
18	Recipients						
19	Newsletters sent						
20	Newsletters opened						
21	Click-throughs						
22	Gifts						
23	Unsubscribes						
24	Email						
25	Recipients						
26	Emails sent						
27	Emails opened						
28	Click-throughs						
29	Gifts						
30	Unsubscribes						
31	Social Media (Facebook)						
32	Page Engagement						
33	Page Engagement Rate						
34	Pages to Watch						
35	Like Sources						
36	Fans Online						
37	Gifts						
38	Visitis to Website						
39	Face-to-face						
40	Calls for Appointments						
41	Appointments Set						
42	Appointments Made						
43	New Donors Acquired						
44	Gifts						
45	New Prospectives Acquired						
46							

— 20 —

Coaching: "I've Got Your Back"

First, let us understand the difference between a coach and a mentor. Coaches help an individual acquire skills. Mentors help develop the individual now and for the future. Coaches are experts in specific fields. Mentors possess more personal experience and knowledge. A coach is task-orientated, while a mentor is relationship-focused.

The focus of **Starting A Ministry** is on teaching and imparting information. So, we'll talk here about how to find a good coach.

You may be wondering precisely what services a coach provides.

Starting A Ministry

Here's a list that is not comprehensive but certainly gives you a good idea of the various assistance one might receive during a typical coaching session:

Clarity – A coach needs to understand the client's vision, how they plan on achieving such goals, and if their skills and gifts are up to the challenges.

- Listen to what's said.
- Ask thought-provoking & clarifying questions.
- Question assumptions.
- Hear what you're not saying.
- Seeing what you're missing in a situation.
- Always being honest.
- Sharing one's opinions and assessments of the client and their situation.

Strategy – The process of creating an action plan to reach one's reasonable, achievable, and measurable goals.

- Asking fundamental questions.
- Brainstorm.
- Serve as a sounding board.
- Creative problem-solving.
- Matching the plan to the client's ability and resources.
- Sharing deep knowledge of a field.

Reinforcement – The process of coming alongside a person to help them achieve their objectives and overcome the obstacles that stand in the way of success.

- Offering encouragement whenever possible.
- Supporting the client along the journey.
- Celebrating the good times.
- Working with the client through difficult situations.

Direction – The guidance and support offered to one while helping them choose the best possible path forward.

- Making the plan understandable.
- Partnering with the client.
- Offering skills training.
- Sharing wisdom & experience.
- Proposing testing and research avenues.
- Presenting ways to measure progress.

Movement – The assistance offered to a person while helping them advance their goals and objectives.

- Accountability.
- Suggest solution methods.
- Offer action plans.
- Helping the client overcome obstacles.

Your homework now is to check off the items in Clarity, Strategy, Direction, Reinforcement, and Movement that are most important to you and seek a coach to provide the necessary assistance.

Is Coaching Paying Dividends?

It's important to have agreed-upon expectations and ways to measure the effectiveness of the coaching.

You're spending valuable time and money to solve problems—are things improving?

Suppose we develop a questionnaire to set expectations before searching for a coach.

Review the Coaching Expectations Questionnaire and answer these 13 questions:

1. Gaining clarity of issues. ____
2. Understanding what is important/what motivates you/the team. ____
3. Exploring and understanding what is holding you/the team back. ____
4. Gaining insight into your/the team's strengths, capabilities, and potential. ____

5. Providing encouragement and support. ____
6. Help define goals. ____
7. Help identify actions and next steps. ____
8. Challenging you/the team with difficult questions. ____
9. Providing honest and direct feedback. ____
10. Making you/the team accountable for project goals. ____

Three additional questions:

11. List the three biggest challenges you/the team overcame in the past twelve months.

12. List the three biggest challenges you/the team hope to overcome in the next twelve months.

13. On a scale of 1 to 10 (with 1 being the least satisfied and ten being the most satisfied), rate how satisfied you are with your project's success. _____

An excellent way to gauge your satisfaction with the coach is to review these expectations occasionally to see if your scores are the same, lower, or higher.

Coaching Expectations Questionnaire (1)

Coaching Expectations Questionnaire

Find additional space after each question so you can be specific in what it is you want the coaching to accomplish. Score on a scale of 1 - 10 where 1 is not at all important and 10 is extremely important:

1. Gaining clarity of issues ____ Explain?
   _____
   _____
   _____

2. Understanding what is important/what motivates you/the team ____ Explain?
   _____
   _____
   _____

3. Exploring and understanding what is holding you/the team back ____ Explain?
   _____
   _____
   _____

4. Gaining insight into you/the team's strengths, capabilities and potential ____ Explain?
   _____
   _____
   _____

5. Providing encouragement and support ____ Explain?
   _____
   _____
   _____

Copyright © 2019 ministryTHRIVE

Coaching Expectations Questionnaire (2)

6. Helping define goals ____ Explain?

   _____
   _____
   _____

7. Helping to identify actions and next steps ____ Explain?

   _____
   _____
   _____

8. Challenging you/the team with difficult questions ____ Explain?

   _____
   _____
   _____

9. Providing honest and direct feedback ____ Explain?

   _____
   _____
   _____

10. Making you/the team accountable for project goals ____ Explain?

    _____
    _____
    _____
    _____

Copyright © 2019 ministryTHRIVE

Coaching Expectations Questionnaire (3)

11. List the three biggest challenges you/the team over came in the past twelve months:

    1. _____
    _____

    2. _____
    _____

    3. _____
    _____

12. List the three biggest challenges you/the team hope to overcome in the next twelve months:

    1. _____
    _____

    2. _____
    _____

    3. _____
    _____

13. On a scale of 1 to 10 (with 1 being the least satisfied and 10 being the most satisfied) rate how satisfied are you with your project's success? _____

    If the satisfaction rating is less than 7 or 8, what specifically is it that causes you to rate your satisfaction lower than a 7?

    _____
    _____
    _____
    _____
    _____

Copyright © 2019 ministryTHRIVE

– 21 –

Conclusion:
Before I Go

S o, what to do now? What's to do with the information shared in **Starting A Ministry**? Will things stay the same? Tomorrow can only be different only if changes are made today.

Is it time to revisit the Purpose, Vision, and Mission statements to ensure clarity? Are the statements memorable? Do people immediately understand the ministry's mission and vision? Does the ministry own a unique position in its nonprofit space, or is it just one of many nonprofits?

Should the ministry make a second attempt to perform additional market research?

Maybe responsibilities deserve another look. Perhaps things can run more smoothly if staff and volunteers are resigned.

The ministry will always discuss budgeting as long as it exists. Can we eliminate any programs or activities? Have we neglected areas that need strengthening and now deserve our attention?

Then there's that whole branding, marketing, PR, and communication piece. Has the best possible job been done in these areas, or is it time to turn things up a notch? Does more expertise need to be brought in?

This author hopes that donor development and fundraising make sense in practical, understandable ways. Ministries will now be better prepared to engage potential donors and be less reluctant to make the *all-important ask.*

Starting A Ministry ends by discussing strategy, planning, and the necessary analysis to ensure the organization achieves the stated goals.

Change Tomorrow! Don't go it alone. There are friends, family, and small group members who want to see you succeed.

Ask for their help.

About the Author

Today, John Leavy enjoys writing and publishing his work toward ministries and non-profits. He is a bestselling author of 21 books and a regular contributor to leading publications and blogs.

Previously, John founded InPlainSite Marketing in 2008, a leader in developing and delivering digital marketing strategies. John consulted and presented to Fortune 100 companies. He specialized in helping businesses understand and leverage emerging web and social media technologies.

Mr. Leavy spent years as an active speaker, trainer, and consultant to company leaders, managers, and technologists at local, national, and international conferences.

On a More Personal Side

John served on the boards of nonprofits for more than a dozen years. He served on leadership councils, as creative director, small group and Bible study leader, and as a volunteer in many other capacities. Today, John's life centers on God, family, church, and community.

John loves spending time with Kay, his bride of 54 wonderful years of marriage. John and Kay have three of the most incredible kids, okay grownups. They have been blessed with eight grandchildren.

BY

JOHN D. LEAVY

FROM THE IGNITION SERIES:

Ignite Your Fundraising

Available at Amazon.com
or wherever books are sold.

BY
JOHN D. LEAVY

FROM THE IGNITION SERIES:

*Ignite Your
Donor Passion*

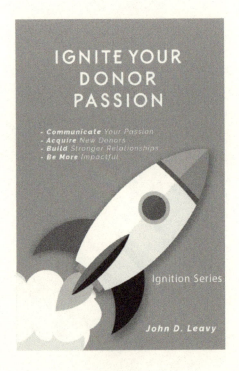

Available at Amazon.com
or wherever books are sold.

BY

JOHN D. LEAVY

FROM THE IGNITION SERIES:

*Ignite Your
Email Campaign*

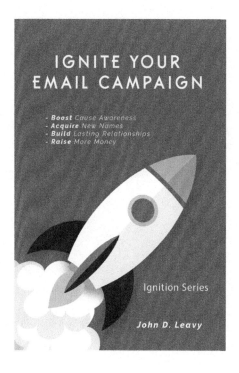

Available at Amazon.com
or wherever books are sold.

Made in the USA
Middletown, DE
14 July 2025

10601049R00128